THE NOT SO TERRIBLE MOVE

A JOAN KAHN BOOK

THE
NOT SO
TERRIBLE MOVE

⌁ or ⌁

WHAT DO YOU DO
WITH THE BED

by
Duvie Clark

HARPER & ROW, PUBLISHERS
New York, Evanston, San Francisco, London

FIRST EDITION

Designed by C. Linda Dingler

Library of Congress Cataloging in Publication Data
Clark, Duvie.
   The not so terrible move.
   1. Interior decoration. I. Title.
NK2115.C58   747   73–4071
ISBN 0–06–010786–3

Contents

Contents

"farmer's syndrome" and into the mood for change
• Using decorating books as practical guides • One
chair as the means to starting out right •
Combining disparate tastes • Buying the bed •
Headboard or not? • Couches • Desks •
Sectional bookcases • Electronic-equipment
purchasing • Picture hanging • Closing off an
exposed kitchen • Possible take-alongs from the
bride's former home • Spending money carefully—
how to get the "no-price-tag look."

The possible decision to stay put • What to give
the ex-husband • The one-wall-at-a-time decorating
job • Odd rules for handling custom painters—
living through a paint job • Getting aid from
doctors, lawyers • Leaning on someone • Ways to
get rid of pieces you don't need • Sleeping in
another room—and why • Reupholstering in bulk
• Antique shopping • Rearranging furniture in the
"tribal fashion." • Buying the bed at a department
store • Bed-linen decisions • The lampshade as
tip-off to new decorating • How the necessity for
comfort gets the place done

The move that can be made too quickly • The
decision to move and why • How to spend the
time between • Finding the right place to go •
How to look for it • Hiring movers • Taking too
much furniture—why it might be wise • Disposing
of the things one loves—with less heartache • Sell
or give away? • The apartment-house-supplied
paint job • A survival furniture arrangement •
The convertible-sofa test • Ordering carpeting and
draperies • Making up for "lost" rooms • Old
furnishings serving new needs

Contents

Contents

shipped, and by what means • The new place and
its needs • The home office and why •
Rethinking telephones, television, bathrooming,
silverware, cooking equipment, dishes, bedding,
dining rooms • How to look at model rooms in
department stores • The way to live together—
separately and better • Techniques for changing
the old life-style with more ease and less emphasis on
money

The newly vacated room—what to do with it and
when • The realization that returning to it will
happen • Getting the room ready • What should
go and what has to stay • Some differences
between girls' and boys' growing rooms • Taking
clues from changing tastes • Painting, lighting,
bedding, curtaining changes—and why • Dividing
one room for a grown son and daughter • Storage
spacing • The "Welcome Home" closet • The
large family—one-at-a-time departures—or putting
covetousness to work, rightly • Can the vacant
room be used as a permanent family den? • How
five different families survived the normal departures
and strange returns

The under-utilized house • The den—right or
wrong? • The husband who looks for sanctuary at
home • The wife who's always waiting • The
reason for making the living room more livable, fast
• Testing furniture arrangements before buying
anything • List of necessities for children's rooms
• Soundproofing • Window blinds that
are different • Building a "collection"—why and
how, for less money • Focal-point madness • The
magic of doors • Vinyl floors • Furniture

Contents

refinishing • Dining-room dining made easier •
Bedroom storage • Looking at other people's
houses • How to get over being afraid of
decorators, how to find one if you need one, and how
to work with one • The wife's very *private haven*—
how one piece of furniture does it—and the
difference it can make • Opening a house to easier
living

THE NOT SO TERRIBLE MOVE

Introduction to a Move

Women, unlike turtles, do not move with their houses on their backs. It just feels that way.

Any moving job is a monumental burden. The business of finding the right place to go, the endless pre-move hesitations, the packing and shipping, the constant redoing and readjusting to the new house; finally, the exhaustion. It's like having major surgery. Without anesthesia or sympathy. (Luckily, we forget physical pain.)

But what about the moving jobs we make when we're aching emotionally?

Those are the terrible moves. The ones all of us face at some time or other in our lives. When we *have to move.* For some usually unhappy reason, when we feel paralyzed. When we've *got to make decisions* anyhow, but we feel we can't.

Here then is a literal guide to getting done with the move and starting a newly designed life. Each very personal story in this book is about a different woman with a different kind of rough move to make. And very probably there is a piece of each of us in every one of them.

No matter what the emotional climate the woman might have been in, there was the bed to think about, or forget; the

1

movers, the painters, the upholsterers all to be dealt with. The pictures that had to be hung. Or rehung.

I know because I was there. I was the hired observer, the interior decorator, who watched and guided them all. Supposedly as a purely objective professional, of course. But I found I could be objective about a chair and not about another woman's problems.

And this book is what came out of it. It's a decorating book —a decorating book without a single diagram or illustration. Because I'm now positive that every woman I've met has her future home in her head. You do, too. Right now, your ideas and desires are waiting to come out. Watch what happens to you when you disagree with a color I'm talking about. You'll have a small interior fight. I'll be talking "green" and you'll think, No, pale yellow is *it!* And you'll be right. Because you'll be responding with that pale yellow room that's been stored away in your mind.

You will know what you want by the simple method of finding out what you *don't* want, by avoiding the mistakes someone else has made, and by finding out *how* to look at other people's houses.

I don't know many other decorators, though I've seen them in showrooms and I've read their books, and seen the rooms they've done. But I know being a decorator requires a great deal of training and an unusual amount of stamina. I would describe a good one as having the mind of Leonardo da Vinci and the agility of a mountain goat. With a touch of the patience of Job.

So despite the fact that I don't know many interior designers, I respect them for what they've been through. If I'm an unusual decorator-designer, if I've written an unusual decorating book —perhaps it's because I've had unusual clients.

If you're about to become a decorator's client, be sure the

decorator is for *you.* You are perfectly right to hire one simply because you like one room in one house he did.

But I can help you get your house in order by *yourself*, if you choose that route. And if, along the way, you get stopped by the choice of a lampshade, or what to do with the coffee table, or where to hang a chandelier, you'll find direction here.

Moving is not *always* a long trip. Sometimes, you must redo the place you're in and feel as if you've moved to a better one. Long haul or not, all you really need is the ability to cope with each detour as it arises. And soon you'll really be home.

1

Suddenly Loverless

"It's over."

Is there one reason for the end of a love affair? No more, I suspect, than there was one reason for the beginning of it. But always the end seems to be sudden. Surely there must have been signs. But one of the lovers didn't want to read them. And, from my experiences with many friends, decorating clients, and a few close relatives, I must say that it's the woman who is nearly always the one who is left stunned and alone.

"It was all so perfect. . . . We were making plans . . . and then *all of a sudden* . . . he moved out. Oh, God."

I heard this lovely, lonely voice on the phone. Could I help by saying that he was suffering, too? No, she had become inverted. Her present agony could only be alleviated by talking about it. Not understanding it. Just talking. And underneath it all, she hoped the phone would ring and it would be he, saying what she wanted to hear.

She wanted him to come back so they could start rebuilding. "I must have done something wrong. . . . I pressed too hard. . . . I could change. . . . I, I . . ." Her voice trailed off.

She needed to have something to touch other than that telephone receiver. She had to see another face reacting. Not just her own bleary image in the bathroom mirror.

I asked her for dinner. It's easy to have an extra person to dinner, especially one who, I thought, wouldn't be able to eat.

She arrived. Not on time. Early. I was at the door to meet her because our doorman had called upstairs to announce that a lady was coming up. We New York apartment dwellers are safeguarded by doormen and/or intercom systems. I'm glad. Not because this always protects us from robbers, but sometimes, as in this case, it allows us to be standing at our open door when our guest arrives.

We embraced. I busied myself hanging up her coat and putting the flowers she had brought into the right vase. She had, meanwhile, headed straight for my couch and wrapped herself in my mohair throw. A small and lovely blanket I bought so that anyone may feel free to lie down on the couch and cover up— or occasionally to cover up the couch in case someone with damp shoes wants to curl up on it.

She started eating pretzels out of a big bowl I always have on my coffee table. I thought of the lovely title of a book by Ludwig Bemelmans. *Are You Hungry Are You Cold.* It asks everything you might ask of someone you care about.

We chatted about nothing much, until we went in to dinner, she still wearing the blanket. I was so anxious to feed her that I was constantly leaving the table to see what else I could find that would fit on a plate.

"Please stay still," she said. "Aren't you going to ask me any questions?"

"Well, yes, but I . . ."

"Go ahead, I'm perfectly fine . . . as you can see."

"Yes, I can see," I said calmly as she wiped her hands on the fringes of the blanket. "I can see that you're going through utterly painful misery. And the only question I can think to ask is, when was the last time you painted your bathroom?"

The Not So Terrible Move

She removed the blanket, folded it, trotted back into the living room, and placed it and herself on the couch.

"Duvie, I'll bet you'd ask a corpse if she liked the floral arrangement you sent! Don't you *ever* stop decorating?"

We started to laugh. And I don't have to tell you that laughter is a lot better than crying. For both the crier and the viewer.

"I want him back! And *you're* making comments about my stupid bathroom."

"Well, if he comes back, you may as well greet him with a nice, freshly painted bathroom."

We kept laughing because we couldn't seem to stop talking about her bathroom. At least I couldn't. And the reason was not really that I'm a compulsive decorator (which I am). A little puzzling?

Not at all. She had to be kept busy and it couldn't be the usual kind of business, which had always ended with her meeting *him*. I think the most consuming, engrossing job in the world is painting an old-style bathroom. Because you can't move the permanent furniture around to make it easy and there's not much tile covering the walls.

By the end of the evening, she was thoroughly convinced that her bathroom was in desperate need of a painting. Since it was blue, it would take two coats to cover, because we decided it might be nicer if it were yellow. And it had better be enamel, which lasts longer. (And is a lot harder to apply.) I told her to buy a roller, which would make the job simpler, and also a brush, because you can't squeeze a roller behind the peculiar conformations of a toilet bowl. It comforted me to know that she owned and knew how to use a ladder. It also comforted me to know that she was an inexperienced painter who had never painted anything bigger than her upper lid with an eye-liner brush.

Of course, the bathroom job didn't cure her heartache.

Though it gave her a chance to phone me daily, usually around 8:00 P.M. Also, it gave her a hair ache. That's not a misprint. She called me—this time, at 2:30 A.M.—with the wildest moan I've ever heard.

"The whole right side of my head is Grapefruit Yellow enamel!" she moaned.

I don't react with anything resembling intelligence at 2:30 A.M.

She slowly and carefully explained that she had overloaded the paintbrush—lifted her arm—and the paint had flopped directly onto her head. She had proceeded to use some turpentine but had gotten scared because her scalp had begun to burn. She had just finished washing her hair in a strong detergent.

"Stop everything," I said. "Get off the phone, and smear your scalp with Vaseline. I'll call someone in the morning, and call you back as soon as I find out what you should do."

"Well, for God's sake—*please* get up *early*. I can't go to work till I hear from you, and I've got to keep my job! And my hair!"

I set my alarm, and at 6:30 A.M. I called another friend. She was as thrilled to hear from me at that hour as I had been at two-thirty. *But* she worked for a beauty-supply firm where I knew they had chemists. I had to get word to the painted painter as soon as I could.

Quickly I explained about the enameled hair, the peculiar type of hair it was (tendency to kink), and the procedures that had taken place since the paint had hit the pate. I also added that the young lady I was concerned about was painting her bathroom at night because she was heartbroken.

There wasn't much of a pause; then my friend said, "I see. Well, it's six-forty-five in the morning—time our chemist got up anyway. I think I'll call him at home."

By seven-thirty my sad friend was applying nail-polish remover to each strand of painted hair, as separately as possible,

7

by using a cotton swab. The Vaseline had been right. She should keep her scalp covered with it, or any bland emollient. Then she was to wash her hair in a mild shampoo. And, if necessary, go through the same process the next day. But she was to keep reapplying the Vaseline between the washings.

It worked out fine for her. Though the chemist had warned that it might not work for everyone.

That night I got my usual call—around eight o'clock.

"Say, Duvie, I've been thinking. A lot of people are working for me for nothing. It's a nice feeling. I mean, that people *care*. If I had a lot of money, I'd hire you and send presents to your friend and her chemist. Would you please let me know their addresses so I can write them thank-you notes?"

She was beginning to reach out. Good.

I knew another thing. Her desire to decorate, and wishing she could hire me as her decorator, meant she was realizing that she wanted to go on living where she was—but differently. It was still going to be her home, whether he came back or not.

Now we could face the actual facts together. She couldn't really redecorate fully, because that takes money, too. She needed decorating help and I could give it to her. As an old friend, I would. But her pride would never allow her to accept it without paying for it. She thought of me as a personal friend, but a *professional* decorator.

Then I remembered. She could sew. I can't. I decided that I needed a gorgeous evening skirt. She would make me a skirt and I would help her make herself a home. Payment in kind is as old and as valid as friendship.

But she wouldn't let me come to her apartment. (I had seen it often before, of course.) She would come to me for advice, or call me on the phone with questions. She was too embarrassed to have visitors because there was still so much of *him* there.

Suddenly Loverless

It had to reach the point where I, or anyone else, would come to *her* home and see *her.*

In spite of her bathroom experience, she became a do-it-yourself decorating nut. (With me as adviser.) She wore a scarf when painting, she bought thin rubber gloves, and she had a jar of Vaseline or liquefying cold cream handy at all times. (More about that later.)

She had very good taste and anyone with very good taste can decorate easily. Right? Wrong. Decorating takes a lot of objectivity and a lot of leg work. But discussing a room or reading about it can give you fresh ideas. A good decorator doesn't impose her ideas on the client; she acts as guide and procurer of workmen, also as a sounding board and, most comforting of all, as the one responsible for any mistakes that are made. And there always are mistakes. Plenty, from lampshade size to couch calamity.

She was making her terrible move *in place;* in other words, redoing a heaven that had turned to hell. To move in place is to take the same four walls and make them seem completely new. It's not much harder than climbing a waterfall.

She and he had loved the beach. She alone, I'm sure, had helped more than any one person to erode the Eastern seashore. She had lovingly picked up every shell and pebble in sight and lugged them home. They were her "collection," as Meissen figurines or Picasso lithographs might be to someone else.

Since I had become her official decorator, I could ask her how she felt about all that beach memorabilia. She might hate the thoughts they brought back. "No," she said, "I've always been dying to *do* something with them." I resisted saying, "Put them back where they came from and help hold back the tides."

We decided to show them off—all together—as any real col-

The Not So Terrible Move

lection should be shown for real impact. She would wash them all, then spray-lacquer them so they'd have luster. The flat pebbles she would glue onto bright green felt. The felt has a backing of self-adhering paper—and she'd do one whole wall in it. It's easy to do and it also meant she wouldn't have to repaint the whole wall.

That wall happened to be the wall behind the bed. Even though the impulse was there to say that her water bed would be fine with beach stuff, neither of us said it.

That bed held not only water but memories, and she softly asked, "How do you get rid of a water bed?"

I wasn't sure. (I've never bought or owned one, so I don't know how you get rid of one.) I suggested she call the place where they'd purchased it, find out how it's drained and dried, and then get rid of it. Most charities won't take bedding. But since a water bed is such a novelty item, probably someone would—for instance, the dorm in a local college. If not, then she'd have to find out from the sanitation department what day they made bulk pickups and have it out on the street then.

She *did* manage to dispose of it. Luckily she got a really lovely couch-bed from her mother, who lived in the suburbs and shipped the couch to her. If that hadn't happened, I would have suggested any floor-sample or bedding sale at a department store. A single bed can cost so little it's amazing. But be sure the mattress is firm, because in small quarters it may also serve as seating space, in which case you'll need bolster cushions for the back and a good cover; and it's nice to know that most department stores have time-payment plans if money isn't available in convenient lumps.

She couldn't wait to gaze at her large shells, so we decided she needed a narrow, six-foot-long shelf that would run the whole length of the wall above her bed. Her particular bed had an upholstered back and arms, so she was safe in leaving just an

18-inch space between the top of the back and the shelf. Especially since the shelf was installed before the couch. She had purchased it from a special shelf store. It was pretend walnut; it had four carved wooden brackets and a workman who came with it. She called to say, "Good thing the couch was free. . . . That shelf was a buy, but the workman charged by the minute! I've got to learn how to do that stuff myself." I couldn't have saved her those "labor pains"; I have them all the time—only more so, because mine are custom-made labor.

Her couch was covered in old, soft pink, and she said she could hardly wait to re-cover it. But when it arrived against that bright green wall—it was the same gentle color as many of her beloved shells.

Her small, adjustable, metal reading lamps (two) could swivel to light up the whole shelf or enable her to read in bed. Decorating magazines. They were the perfect reading for her. They rarely have people pictured in their model rooms, because that would cover up too much of the furniture being shown. So she would get no pangs from seeing family groupings.

Her one-room-kitchenette-bath apartment also had windows. She had painted around the window frames and done all the other exposed walls in white. But she didn't want the old draperies.

There were Venetian blinds, however, so she washed them in her tub and hung them up wet, so the tapes would dry straight. Then we planned to cover her windows with plants.

First she would have to talk to the plant man on her corner. He told her what plants to get and how to pot them. There were, naturally, some of her pebbles in the base plates of the clay pots on the floor. The plant pots that hung from the ceiling were installed with special bolts after she had consulted with the salesman in the nearest hardware store. She installed them herself, with tools she had bought. She told me, "The plants are

11

little now, but they'll do well. . . . Not too near the heater, he said, but with plenty of water, they'll even add some humidity to the room. But they'll need lots of care." She had it to give.

Her closets were stuffed, she told me.

I knew she had spent a lot of money on clothes when he was with her. But I also knew she was very neat. She was not a closet-stuffer type.

"I still have a lot of his things," she said. She told me he'd taken most of his clothes, but there were the skis and poles and the books she'd had to shove away when she started the big paint job. And the things he'd given her.

"Are you at the point now where you can send them back to him?"

She knew where he was. He had never given up his old apartment, which he'd shared with another man.

We talked it over. She wouldn't call him. She never had since he'd left. (That was an amazing strength.) So she would get his things together—cartons for his books (not big cartons, because you can't lift them), boxes for whatever was boxable, the skis and poles tied together. She'd take a cab and drop them off with his superintendent or doorman. She would have to write him a note. We decided it would say: "Dear _____, I'm sure you need the things I'm having delivered to you on [the date and the day, not the time]. Be sure someone is there to receive them. Hope all goes well with you. Best," and her signature would be the nickname he had given her.

Her heart would be in that note. But it had to be done, and with the good manners she'd always had. It would also give him an opening if he wished to use it. (I never asked her if he called or wrote to thank her. She would have told me. But there was nothing to tell.)

Then, about the presents he had given to her. There were several fine record albums, a portable stereo set, some graphic art (not expensive, but mutually chosen), a lighted digital clock, some pretty but not costly jewelry.

"You know those were given to you to keep, so sending them back would accomplish nothing," I said. "I don't think you'll be listening to the music you enjoyed together, because you have too much good sense, though later maybe you will. But to have a stereo set is a delight. And you need that lit digital clock so you can be sure it's 2:30 A.M. when you call *me!*"

We also felt that since she was redecorating, she probably wouldn't be using the art works they had chosen. She'd store them until she really wanted to display them. The gift and the giver don't remain perpetually interlocked. Something that was lovely once remains lovely, even if it has to be hidden for a while.

She had seen an all-Spanish kitchen in one of her decorating magazines—one of those totally appointed, enormous paradises. But, like anyone who really wants ideas and knows how to get them, she had gotten the "feel" from the photograph. By using Spanish tile stick-it-on-the-wall-yourself paper, she was living in that glorious kitchen she had seen.

And she told me something *I* didn't know. If the adhesive-type paper gets a bubble in it after it's applied, just stick a straight pin in the bubble and it goes flat again.

She said that her lined-up white kitchen cabinets and appliances looked spanking new against the bright paper. But not very Spanish. So I told her to bring me one of the drawer pulls and one of the cabinet handles. They were the usual chrome and, luckily, standard size. Replaced with inexpensive black wrought-iron ones, they made the whole kitchen into her own version of Andalusia.

Of course, her hardware store had supplied the miraculous ironwork and the instructions. She became a fellow-worshiper of hardware stores. Find a good one, and you have a great source of comfort. They give you the right-size nails, hammers, bolts, and they always seem to know the address of the nearest lumberyard. The kind of lumberyard that doesn't think everyone is a former logger or cabinetmaker.

Now she knew where to get precut shelving in clear pine. (That's without knotholes and splinters, so you don't need an electric sanding machine.) They had shelf brackets, unfinished, to match the ones that had almost finished off her budget. They told her how many brackets she'd need to hold a shelf up (over two feet long means more than two brackets unless you like U-shaped shelves). She stained them walnut.

She was adding random shelving to her pebbled green felt wall. Some of the pebbles were falling off, despite the epoxy cement she'd used, and were clonking her prized shell shelf. So now the extra shelves held the errant pebbles, plus wood carvings, white marble obelisks, opened paper fans, and colored-glass bottles.

Since she'd stopped buying clothes and putting together fancy dinners *à deux*, she used her money to buy things for her home. The Oriental import stores, the junk shops led her farther and farther afield. She walked off her weekends.

She had bought a semi-decent mahogany drop-leaf table. The kind that can stay narrow with both leaves down, or square with one open, or rectangular with the two leaves up. From her description, it should also do something else. Get refinished.

"Before you start stripping that complicated thing, try using some dark-tone furniture and scratch-cover polish. The liquid is easy to apply. Your hardware store has it, I'll bet." (I had noted certain symptoms of exhaustion. She kept falling asleep on my couch while I was talking about *her* home. That's a sure sign of fatigue.)

The dark liquid worked. She could postpone perfection, as

well as total exhaustion. The table, opened to its square size, stuck out from the long wall opposite her couch setup. We agreed it would look more inviting open than shut. (And I hoped she'd start inviting people in to start eating at that table.)

Of course she owned chairs. Exactly three. One club chair covered in coarse, faded brown tweed—with square, short, exposed legs. And two of the much beloved, overbought, but cheap Italian Chiavari chairs. The kind with tall, thin ladder backs, slender legs, and rush woven seats.

Two dining-room chairs don't a party make.

"Do you like the two Chiavari chairs?"

She looked at me, sighed, and said, "I adore them. Except for a couple of things. They're creaking. And they're not Queen Anne style."

She couldn't afford Queen Anne–style chairs, even unfinished, unless she suddenly married into royalty.

If you want to buy chairs, look at the ads in your newspaper. Especially Sunday ads. There are stores all over that sell chairs and tables. And tables and chairs. They buy by the shipload and sell in the same quantities. Their prices make the word "wholesale" sound expensive. They're the biggest bargain purveyors since the group who decided to sell Manhattan Island for twenty-four dollars' worth of beads.

She went, she saw, and she bought four bentwood chairs with cane seats. In a dark wood finish. She said they looked curvy, they felt comfortable, and she would eventually make flat foam-rubber cushions for their seats—and for the relief of guests' bottoms. They *are* classic chairs, and their looping curves reminded her of Queen Anne chairs. Her imagination was the only thing that counted—I was decorating by remote control. Her house was taking shape in her head and coming to life around her.

Now her dining setup was complete. Except for the lighting. In her previous setting, candlelight on a card table had been the order of the evening.

Now she said, "Duvie, all my life I've wanted a crystal chandelier."

"You mean you've never wanted a diamond tiara?"

She got the idea. This was not the time of her life to get a crystal chandelier. Cheap ones are ugly. Stealing is illegal. But we had to have lighting, and she said she'd think about a crystal chandelier for the future. (The fact that she was starting to believe she *had* a real future was nice.)

First, she'd get a mirror. At least as wide as the table. She'd hang it on the wall, from tabletop level on upward. It would reflect the length of the table, making it seem twice as long. Mirrors reflect light during the day, as well as at night.

The mirror she found had good glass. Which is important if you're going to be staring into it a lot. It also had a very carved wood frame which was battered to pieces. That worried her. She investigated plastic wood to fill in the whorls and swirls. I said, "Get out the wall paint you've got left and paint the frame to match the wall; nobody will even notice the missing pieces." She had already hung the long mirror, vertically. (That means up and down, and there are some really brilliant people who do not know the difference between vertical and horizontal. Remember the horizon is flat. Those who were raised in mountainous country may *never* learn the difference.)

I told her to put her liquefying cold cream on the glass edges of the mirror, as close to the frame as she could. This would keep the paint from permanently adhering to the glass, enabling her to remove any that did get on the glass without having to use a razor blade on the mirror. (The sound of which is enough to drive some people incurably insane.) So she slopped white paint on the recently hung mirror on the newly painted white wall.

Suddenly Loverless

(Between the cold cream and a little strong soap and water—and the occasional use of a piece of steel wool—she got the excess paint off all the exposed edges of the mirror.)

But then the paint hit the table, and she hit the roof! And the phone. I was home. I yelled, "Quickly, throw some cold cream on the spots on the table!"

She called me back. The paint had come off with a little fingernail urging. Then she just reapplied the scratch-cover liquid to the tabletop.

Table and mirror and chairs were doing well. Now we needed a lamp to put on the table right in front of the mirror (which would look normal even if the table was eventually folded flat against wall). Also her lamplight would be doubled because the mirror would reflect it.

She was all for buying a large, round, lowish lamp she had seen. It was pale pink, she told me, and had a pleated white plastic shade that would let the light through. But when we talked about it, she changed her mind because she realized it would take up too much table surface and block the view into the mirror.

"Go to the lamp department of a good department store and look for the table that says 'Specials.' " (They nearly always have them. Sometimes the shades are a little battered or they're the remaining unbroken lamp of a former pair.)

She went to several stores. Then, after about two weeks, she arrived at my house with her lamp. Strangely enough, it was the first thing she'd bought that I'd ever really seen. I would have told her I adored it even if I hated it. Because I knew it was a "No Return" and because she had chosen it.

(No, I don't make a practice of lying to clients. No good decorator should. But this was a special case. Come to think of it, each client is a special case. I guess that's why I decorate. And sometimes lie.)

17

The Not So Terrible Move

The lamp? Truly a beauty. It was tall and slender. It looked like a cathedral candlestick made of silvery Mexican tin. She'd had to buy a shade. (That's why the lamp was on sale; its shade was mangled.) She had bought a lampshade in the same store under the guidance of the lampshade saleslady and *with* the lamp. Which is the best way to do it. The shade was flared at its base and it was white almost-silk. I told her to get one of those pinkish-tinted light bulbs. I knew she wanted that pink of the sea shells.

With the silvery glitter of the tall slim lamp against the mirror, she had attained the look of crystal. And since the lamp didn't block the mirror she could sometimes put low glass bowls on each side of it filled with flowers or fruits or mints.

Only the club chair was left. She looked it over for me and said it was as sturdy as the Rock of Gibraltar, and also looked like it. Huge.

"Is it comfortable?"

"Wow, yes," she answered. "I'm always curled up in it, watching TV or sewing up old pantyhose."

The club chair needed no repair—and it was comfortable. From what she told me, all it needed was a slipcover. It was being placed in her window-garden area—against all whites and greenery. (Not directly *under* any of those hanging pots, ever.) I told her to go to one of those mill-outlet stores or fabric mill-end places, and to choose a sturdy slipcover fabric with a white background and a greenhouse-type print. Leafy, maybe floral, or with an openwork pattern featuring bright green against white. (She could spotproof-spray the fabric.) The important thing was that it should "disappear" in that area by becoming a visual part of it. Its size would seem to diminish if the fabric became a part of the background.

"I don't think I can make a slipcover," she said.

"I know for sure that you can't."

Suddenly Loverless

A well-made slipcover is like upholstery. It must be cut to fit beautifully. That takes a professional and money. Good club chairs are costly, so it would be worth it. I told her to get in touch with the upholstery shop nearest her—tell them the chair's measurements and get an approximate price for the job. Also, to ask them how much fabric she'd need. She should buy the fabric immediately if she found one she loved. The outlet places usually don't have a lot of any particular item, so you must buy it when you see it. Then she could wait to have the job done if her money was running out.

Meanwhile I told her to buy large brass casters and install them on the club chair's stocky wooden legs. These big wheels enable you to roll a heavy chair; so she could have comfortable seating anywhere in her room or angle the chair in any direction. The slipcover would hide them from sight. (Though in case of upholstery or the lack of a skirted covering, the casters themselves are attractive.)

"If I put that big chair on wheels, it'll roll itself across the room and stop against the nearest wall or go straight into the bathroom!"

She had waxed her dark wooden floors. She didn't have a rug. I rarely suggest wall-to-wall carpeting in what will doubtless be temporary quarters. She needed an area rug.

"Really, a smallish rug will do—in front of your pink couch. The wooden floors left exposed will be a blessing for your dining-room section. No bouillabaisse on the rug. And it'll stop your rolling easy chair from total escape." Besides, if you don't want it to roll too easily, you can always put rubber pads under the wheels. (Some of the casters have lock-in-place mechanisms.)

She liked the idea of an area rug. We decided a 6' × 9' would be plenty big enough. With the long part running along the floor in front of the couch. The six-foot width would allow easy movement of the dining-room chairs because it wouldn't be too near them. And—ah, yes—she would love an antique Persian. Once again, I suggested marriage: to an antique Persian gentleman.

"Have you cased your mother's house on the rug situation?" I asked.

"Well, yes."

"And the answer was 'Nothing doing'?"

Right. Especially, when her mother realized that she had also had to send along the bed linens for the couch-bed. (Without them, our friend would have had to spend a bundle on sheets, pillowcases, blankets—a hidden, but very real expense.)

I suggested watching the papers for rug sales at department stores. And that she approach the rug salesman in the store in a completely honest and open fashion. Something like, "Sir, I am poverty-stricken. What's the cheapest rug you've got that doesn't have to last forever? A two-year stint will do just fine." (She had two years to go on her lease.)

She called me from the store. She was whispering in a phone booth. "I got such a bargain—I feel like a crook!" Funny, I thought, purchasers of rugs usually feel the salesman is a crook. It was indeed refreshing.

Her 6' × 9' rug was a copy of a Persian rug. Made in India. She described it: deep ivory, with a central oval of flowers and leaves in shades of greens, blues, and pinks; the four corners had more of the pattern kind of drifting inward—the border continued the small flowers and leaves.

She was describing an Aubusson rug.

I smiled. "The rug sounds beautiful, but I've got to tell you something. Your Persian is a copy of a French rug, made in India."

"To me it's a Persian." And, she said, the few stains and discolorations made it look truly antique. Also, she could pay it off. I made her rush right back and order a pad to go under it

20

—no area rug should ever be put down for even five minutes without a lining under it. Unless you want someone to collect your life insurance quickly. They slide as if they were on fifteen sets of casters.

The day the rug arrived, she called me and said, "Duvie, I'm in love." I was too speechless to answer. She continued, "I mean, I'm in love with my apartment. . . . I love to walk into it."

Eight months had passed since her first visit to me, when I'd forced her into her bathroom to do a job she didn't know how to do.

"I want you to come to a party at my house!" She *said* it. And it was the one party of the year everybody tries not to give. New Year's Eve!

We walked into a house whose door was opened by the prettiest hostess in the world.

The room was like the inside of a glorious sea shell, glowing and pearly. The plants were a tropical delight. The greens and pinks were the loveliest signs of nature. It was like taking a vacation.

On her gleaming table were the good things to eat that made you feel as if you were at a surprise picnic. Her big plastic punch bowl was afloat with fruits, and bubbled like the incoming tide. That was champagne punch, I guess.

I drank a lot of her punch. So I dared to ask her: "This *was* a terrible move wasn't it? But it's so . . ."

She stopped me. "It was a *terrible* move? Maybe. But it moved all the loose pieces of *me* back together again. I'm whole, I'm home, I'm home free."

2

The Bewildered Bride-to-Be

There is nothing nicer in the world than getting a phone call announcing an upcoming marriage. But the little shocker that came along with the call I got was that *I* was to be one of the wedding gifts!

Here's how it went:

"Hi, Mrs. Clark, remember me? I'm Cherry Lee. You decorated our house and I'm getting married and my folks said they'd be glad to hire you to do my new apartment. I can take some of the things you put in my old bedroom and Mom said I can have the dining-room buffet and Dad said he'll pay your fee. And how are you?"

"I'm fine, thank you." But I was also puzzled.

I was puzzled because I couldn't remember ever having done a Lee house. But how can you say to someone who obviously knows you, and whose parents' house you obviously decorated, that you can't remember a thing about it?

How? Well, I said, "Cherry Lee, I really am fine and I hope you are, but I'm positive that you have the wrong Clark, because I don't know a thing you're talking about. I never did a house for any people named Lee."

"It's Cherry Lee—Cherry Lee Simon! Milt and Minnie Simon's daughter. I *know* you're the right Clark—you're Duvie. You used nail polish to make my little chandelier the same bright pink as the roses on my wallpaper!"

Cherry Lee. Nail polish. Cherry Lee Simon. Cherry Lee Simon was only twelve years old.

"What are you doing getting married—you're only twelve years old—aren't you?"

It seemed that a little time had passed. Something like eight years.

I began to age almost immediately. I had become a second-generation decorator. I was being handed down like a piece of silver.

I asked about her parents' health and other items that entered my head as I went back in time.

"Say, Cherry Lee, are you like your mother? I loved her, but honestly, *she* couldn't make a decision to open an umbrella in a rainstorm."

"No. I remember you once told Mom you were a decorator, not a cemetery—that you weren't selling *perpetual care!*"

This child remembered almost everything I had said or done. More important, she disapproved of her mother's inability to make decisions. *She* wanted her new apartment done fast.

Done fast, so that it would be livable fast. Also, she knew *exactly* what she wanted. But, mostly, she wanted me.

"Duvie, I want you because of the room you gave me when I was little. You wouldn't let Mom come with us when we shopped. You said I was your client because you were doing my room."

I remembered that. She had been such a gawky girl and I had wanted her to have a romantic room. And her dad had briefed me on the price ranges. It had been a wonderful day. She had tramped alongside me, carrying all my shopping bags, and we put together a room that made her feel like a fairy princess. I even remembered lunch—she ate enough food to sustain a rhinoceros.

And so she was to be my client again. This time she was building her own apartment rather than her own bedroom, but Daddy was still going to foot the bills. I always charge a fee for my services, plus commission, which is a specified percentage over the wholesale price of any purchases made. My charging a basic fee enables the client to do some wholesale shopping on her own.

I'm the kind of decorator who likes it when a client has a wholesale contact. I like it for several reasons, all of them selfish. My fee makes it possible for me to:

1. Act cheerful and helpful in a showroom even when I know I'm not going to make any commission.

2. Get to know new sources and the owners of said sources of merchandise.

3. Find out the *real* base price of some items. As you might imagine, the relative-client gets a cheaper price than a decorator does. She gets the price that a dealer would get (like a store owner). I have seen the same table sell for three different wholesale prices!

4. Not be held responsible if the legs fall off the table purchased, or the carpet folds up into a pleated mess, because I didn't make any commission on it, it didn't come from my source, and my workmen had nothing to do with it.

I would be very happy if I never had to earn a nickel in commissions and just worked on a plain, flat-fee basis. The fee, naturally, depends on several things. How big the house or apartment and how long I think the job will take. Also, how much furniture the client owns at the beginning of the job. (If the place is already jammed, I can work on an hourly basis. I truly love that.)

The Bewildered Bride-to-Be

My new, old, young client, Miss Cherry Lee Simon, was anxious to get going. She was so enthusiastic and full of glee.

"Oh, Duvie," she purred, "I'm marrying the most wonderful boy in the world."

Now, *there's* a description that really lets you in on the type of man you're going to have as the husband half of the new team.

"What's his name, how old is he, and what does he do?" I asked.

"Oh, he's still in school, he's going to be a biochemist in a couple of years, and then he'll go on to graduate school and get his doctorate in microbiology, and then he'll go on and become—"

"Excuse me, Cherry Lee, but what's his name? You know . . . like what do you call him?"

"His name? Oh, Tom. Thomas Bergmann."

Anytime I'm on the phone, I doodle. I draw all over anything available. I found myself drawing Cherry Lee Simon's new name. In other words, designing her monogram. Cherry Simon would be Cherry Simon Bergmann. Her monogram? cBs. (She was not only becoming a wife, she was becoming a television network.)

"Well, Cherry Lee, I can tell you right off that you can forget about monogrammed towels. Unless you want your guests to think they've ambled into a TV channel instead of a bathroom."

She hesitated, wrote down what I told her—and almost exploded. I swear she was ready to call off the wedding. I don't know why it is, but brides are absolutely dotty on the subject of monogrammed towels.

I am always delighted when the initials turn out to be unprintable. I think monogrammed towels are dreadful, unnecessary, usually ugly, and uncomfortable to dry with because the initials are scratchy. Besides, if your guests don't know your name by the time they're in your bathroom, they shouldn't be there.

It follows that I'm not too thrilled with other types of towel printing. Those cute terry cloths marked: "His," "Hers," "Yours," "Theirs," "Ours," "Its," "Whose?" They all fairly shatter me. (And they are the world's most popular wedding presents, I'd guess.)

Wedding presents. I would be working with a couple of poor unfortunate people on the receiving end of wedding presents. Whatever the current craze—be it bonbon dishes, table lighters, silver "silent butlers"—everyone would be sending them duplicates and triplicates of the great unnecessaries. (Why don't people just send a large supply of paper towels, thirty-six boxes of cleansing tissues, or twelve 100-watt light bulbs?)

"Cherry Lee, before we make our first date to meet here at my place, I've got to know, have you had any showers yet? Do friends still do that kind of thing? And are people asking you what you both want for the house?"

Well, it turned out that the girls in her office (yes, she had a job) were planning a little "something." And her relatives had started asking what she'd like in the way of gifts.

"Really, Duvie," she said, finally slowing down, "I don't know what I want. Tom says I should just get it done. He works so hard he's exhausted."

I made an appointment with her for the first possible free day she had. Saturday. Which was the next day.

I spent the whole evening making a list—a Bridal Thinking List:

She has to ask for things she wants and needs.

She has to know her "customers"—how much they can afford to spend.

The Bewildered Bride-to-Be

I have to find out or inspire her color scheme, quickly.

Tom's taste *has* to become involved. (He may be too exhausted to think now, but he will react with energy later if he hates what she chooses.)

If we get the gifts fairly under control, she can save a lot of money and closet space (because she won't have to hide them until the giver shows up).

I have to ask if she's listed herself with those bridal registries some stores have. So that people can give the bride a teaspoon in her chosen pattern. Or a soup bowl.

With those items checked off, we could then discuss the apartment she had mentioned. It sounded as if she had already chosen one. Then with *her* budget, or Daddy's, firmly planted in my mind, we could go on. This would be an almost starting-from-scratch job. Maybe she'd have a couple of pieces from her maiden home, but, remembering Mama Minnie, I might have to help replace them.

After I said my prayers, I added a P.S.: "Dear Father, please put a thought in Cherry Lee's head that *I* forgot. Please tell her to bring Tom with her tomorrow. But *not* Minnie."

I shall not say another word about the power of prayer.

But the next day arrived and it was Saturday, as expected.

And, at the appointed hour, it was Cherry Lee and Tom, as requested.

Cherry Lee and I embraced, Tom stood behind her, filling the doorway. I stepped back to look at little Cherry Lee. She was still little and still young and sweetly beautiful. Tom was so handsome I almost swooned.

They didn't need a decorated apartment. All they needed was a frame for themselves.

After the usual amenities, I sat down in a nearby chair and

said, "There was one question I forgot to ask Cherry Lee last night. When's the wedding?"

Tom answered, "Right after exams in mid-June."

A June bride!

The June groom then added, "Look, I hate to do this, but I've got to be at the lab in about an hour, so could you take a look at these plans of our apartment?" And he handed me the folded floor plan.

Floor plans: a floor plan is a diagramed view-from-above of a room or a series of rooms. I think they're for the birds. Only a bird is accustomed to gazing at spaces from aboveground. The average human never enters a room through the ceiling, and therefore doesn't have any idea of what a room really looks like if he depends on a floor plan. They are useful to those of us who need measurements and need to know construction peculiarities. Anybody who tries to arrange furniture *solely* depending upon a floor plan is guaranteed to have a room he'll never recognize upon entering it.

You see a room *in toto* only once. And that's when you walk into it. From then on, you see only one section at a time. Sure, the floor plan will tell the future dweller that he has a twenty-foot wall opposite a ten-foot wall with a ten-foot opening leading to a dining area. But, the future dweller might wish to order a twenty-foot sofa and a ten-foot breakfront just to get it over with. And that, indeed, would be a joyous and swift furnishing job. Of course, neither piece would go through the average door. So it's best to come down off the ceiling and do a room from standard floor position—the kind one assumes when standing in a room and looking around.

Cherry Lee and Tom had the floor plan of their future 3½-room apartment. It would be available to them in April. Meanwhile, since it was now mid-February, they wanted to use the plan to order their furniture. It can be done that way. A lot of motels, hospitals, nursing homes, and restaurants are furnished that way. It therefore follows that any home or apartment furnished by the floor-plan-only technique will resemble a motel, hospital, nursing home, or restaurant. (I like to visit a nice motel but I surely wouldn't want to live in one permanently.)

"Can we *see* the apartment now, or one like it—maybe even a model?"

I asked the question not sure the building was fully constructed. To view a model apartment is to view the most expensive version of the space you're going to rent. You must blind yourself to the elaborate wallpaper and electrified wall brackets, and only look at the space.

Luckily, the apartment they were to take over in April was now occupied by friends. A married couple who were about to become a threesome—or maybe more.

Tom could hardly wait for me to see the apartment. He was very fond of the way it was presently furnished, and thought Cherry Lee and he should repeat the same theme.

That is not unusual. Many people view furnished living space and can only see it in its present form. (If the couch is in the middle of the long wall, they see it always being that way.) These people are not suffering from lack of imagination. They are suffering from "farmer's syndrome": anything that's planted must have roots. To them, all the furnishings are rooted to the floor. Forever.

Often when I have new clients, I start by taking them through my apartment or lending them a decorating book. The great decorating books are put out by *House & Garden* (for the wealthier set), *Better Homes & Gardens* (the slightly less rich groups), or any one of the series of *Decoration* published by French-European Publications, Inc. (These are for castle dwellers, but their illustrations are caviar—sumptuous, delicious, and guaranteed to snap anyone out of visual apathy.)

The Not So Terrible Move

By using this book technique, I can find out a few very important things. What colors are most appealing to the new clients. What their reaction to a room is. Because a reaction is all one should get from looking at a picture of a perfect room. And what kind of accessories they prefer. Because a room that is really budget can become dazzling with a couple of truly interesting accessories, well placed.

Another thing I find out is whether these new clients return books. A good decorating book can cost anywhere from five dollars to fifty dollars, sometimes even more. (Some can be picked up at discount bookshops, and the great ones printed as far back as 1949 are still great.) Aside from the ghastly high price of these tomes, anyone who doesn't return a book doesn't return to my house very often.

Tom didn't show much reaction to my apartment. He followed me around and made a few comments. He admired my clock-radio, made in Japan and about as unusual as a large bar of soap. He liked a plain, tall, squarish white marble lamp with a black paper shade that was next to my bed. Which I had purchased simply because it was on sale at a store near me and could hold a light bulb. He liked a Peter Max poster in my hall, available anyplace posters are sold.

Clearly, he fell into the category of book borrower. When he left shortly, he had under his arm my 1960 edition of *House & Gardens' Complete Guide to Interior Decoration*. He was very worried about returning it. I said we'd meet soon and he could return it then. Which was a double-pronged move on my part.

You see, I had to get *him* involved in furnishing their new apartment. I didn't want him shopping with us constantly; he didn't have the time and most men find it a monumental bore. But starting a brand-new house for a brand-new couple can be the start of a marriage built on sharing. Any other kind of marriage shouldn't start at all.

The Bewildered Bride-to-Be

Cherry Lee stayed on with me. She galloped around my place enthusiastically admiring everything in sight. And dropping ashes all over everything.

"Cherry Lee, how long have you been smoking so heavily?"

"I only started smoking recently."

"When?"

"Right after we, uh, got engaged."

Now, everybody knows nobody should smoke at all. I know that and, of course, I still smoke. But I've been smoking since I was sixteen. I figure that the next time *I* get engaged I'm going to stop smoking.

I got her back to the couch, armed with a huge ashtray and a matching drink. She started one of her solo talking jags.

"Duvie, I love him very much and the folks love him and he's so bright and handsome. Life is going to be so wonderful. But I'm tired and I'm afraid I'll choose the wrong things and he won't like it and he says he doesn't care, anything's all right as long as the apartment stays the way it is and I get everything done. And *I hate it!* It's terrible to move. . . . Did you know that? Can you believe it? Am I crazy?"

The truth was, yes, she was temporarily crazy. And the truth is, any move is terrible. Even if you're in love and getting married. Her tiredness was defeating her. She needed to rest and make no decisions. Just float for a while. Which was impossible.

"Look, Cherry Lee, let's just take things easy. You've got plenty of time and I've worked out this little list to straighten out your bridal-gift decisions. Let's talk about that first. Okay?"

Here, finally, was something she could hold on to. It didn't require any big decisions and most of the work could be done on the phone. She'd just talk to friends and relatives or any other poor soul who'd got to give somebody a wedding gift. (As

I've said, receiving rotten wedding gifts is bad, but shopping for one is a shade worse.)

She was listed with the bridal registry of a large well-known jewelry, silver, dishware, and gimcrack store. Their prices matched their name in topflight elegance. She had registered herself in their silver-flatware division as being the bride desirous of a silverware pattern that looked a lot like stainless steel. Her reasoning was if it *looked* like stainless steel she wouldn't have to polish it as often as silver.

"Cherry Lee, do you want to have that silverware for the rest of your life?"

"No. But silver is so hard to clean. I want something that'll—"

"Silver flatware is hard to clean if you let it get tarnished. And mostly it gets tarnished from *not* being used. If you use it very often, you wash it very often and it won't need hard polishing except occasionally. So choose a pattern you really want and ask if the knives have soldered handles. If they do, remember you can't put them in a dishwasher, because the solder will melt. Solder is the heavy glue substance that holds handle to blade. But it won't kill you to wash the knives in the sink. You don't have to choose the fanciest, most expensive pattern in the world, but neither should you choose the simplest, cheapest one, just to get it over with."

She knew the pattern she *really* liked. She would call the store and tell them. So that took care of that.

The fine china was a different story. She had chosen a delicate porcelain service that would cost about $175 a place setting. Not only was she unlikely to amass even one complete place setting, but she would probably store such china away and never use it for fear of breakage. (The reason there are completely intact dinner services for twelve available in antique porcelain is very simple: our ancestors didn't use them, either, except for baronial birthdays.)

For years I have tried to convince clients, friends, and relatives to *use* their good dishes. I've told them to put a service for four in the kitchen, so's it's handy. I've said they'd survive a broken teacup. I've talked on and on. To no avail. It stays in the breakfront until somebody celebrates getting a year older or dies. So I've given up. Certainly a young bride didn't need any extra traumas.

But there *are* dishes that are extremely handsome and durable. (And they're made by the same prestigious companies who make the nervous-breakdown crockery.) This fine china holds up in a dishwasher, looks lovely though it's weightier, and can be used for breakfast, lunch, and dinner. That's the kind to get. Later, the husband and wife may take a cruise and perhaps start picking up English bone china or the like. Or their parents will hand over part, or all, of the good dishes they got when *they* were married.

Cherry Lee reacted to my china tale with complete comprehension. As a matter of fact, Tom had had fits when he'd heard about the dishes she'd signed up for. Said he could get an electron microscope for the price of a set. So *that* pattern would be switched at the store, too. You could get the kind I had spoken of there, as well, and it could be acquired by anyone who wanted to spend anywhere from about five dollars on up, depending on what piece they chose.

I told her to use her family and *their* friends for the pricier gifts. And not to forget those necessities that can keep you on a time-payment plan forever: vacuum cleaner, blender, toaster, percolator, clock-radio, extra blankets, and bed linens. All the unglamorous expensives.

The Not So Terrible Move

Cherry Lee was fast getting hold of herself. She munched pretzels.

I continued my decorative lecture and inquisition.

"Say, didn't you have a very rich aunt and uncle . . . Auntie Mame and Uncle Vanya, or something like that?"

"I think you mean Aunt Bess and Uncle Herman . . . yup, I've still got them. She's been after me about a present. I hate to ask for money, but she's talking about giving us a solid-silver tea service!"

"Okay, do you and Tom like TV?"

"Uh, yes."

"So how about asking your lovely kinfolk to give you a color-TV set? A nice, large-screen portable. Not one of those things in a big carved wooden casket."

I was referring to TV built into large credenzas. Well-engineered color-television sets and even stereo-sound systems are often packed into "custom"-designed home-entertainment units. The engineers who design the electronic equipment are admirable and well trained. The "Old World craftsmen" who design the cabinets that hold all this simplified gadgetry were trained to build Viking ships. Buying a gorgeous piece of furniture that will hold the equipment you choose is one thing. But buying the ready-made "totals" is an investment in a huge hunk of wooden bulk with all the quality of a bunch of orange crates.

I believe in good sound and viewing equipment. TV, record players, AM-FM radios and amplifiers, cartridge decks for cassettes, and fine speakers are desirable. But they don't all have to be in one spot. They can be on shelves or enclosed in small cabinet space. Spend money on the equipment itself, not on the boxes they can come in. Especially if you're just setting up housekeeping.

There was only one area of presents we hadn't touched upon. The really inexpensive ones. The ones she and Tom would get the most of, because they had lots of young friends (and a few not-so-rich older ones).

Housekeeping for Cherry Lee would be only a part of her life. She was holding on to her job, she was starting a marriage, she would have to entertain—*and* keep house. So I suggested that for inexpensive presents she request:

A set of stainless-steel flatware. Simple and heavyweight. Purchasable, too, in open stock (in other words, available constantly and in separate pieces)—just choose a moderately priced one in a semi-decent store. Very cheap stainless steel means bent spoons and flaccid forks.

Mugs for coffee or tea. Ask for them in white or solid colors. They last, and are only one piece to wash.

Attractive place mats. Bright plastic ones can be very effective. Heavy woven ones are easy to wash.

Large bowls. In colored lacquer or clear glass (ovenproof) or in any of the heavyweight plastics that range from clear, through smoky, and into bright colors. Great for the ever-present one-dish meals, vast salads—and beautiful for wine punches or fruits.

Ashtrays. Large and small ones. Again in bright colors. Even nonsmokers have guest smokers.

Stackable wine racks. Wine is served almost constantly today. And it's brought as a present to almost every dinner party. A set of wine racks next to each other or stacked up is lovely to look at and keeps wine correctly.

Glassware. Just say whether you like simple ones or fancy ones. Request water glasses, or wineglasses, or champagnes, or brandies. And let the chips fall where they may. The glasses will do the same thing, so you're never stuck for long with ugly glassware.

I kept referring to color and bright color in those gift suggestions. Every time I did, Cherry Lee herself turned pale. I sensed there was a problem with color. The most likely problem was that she and Tom did not share "favorite" colors.

"I know this will shock you, Duvie, but Tom and I agree on everything—world affairs and birth control, and we even like the same foods. *But* he likes all beigy colors and I like bright blues and sunny colors. It's a mess."

"No, it's not a mess. It's normal. So you'll tell your inquisitive callers you're using beige and earth tones and bright touches of blues, golds, yellows; and if they've got to be directed, tell them black or white. This way, you'll both be pleased because these presents aren't your furniture or your walls."

A large, contented sigh was heard.

I got her coated and gloved and reminded her to take my list with her and attend to it.

Panic struck her at the door. "When will I see you again— when do we go see the new place? . . . What do I—"

I stopped her before she finished the last question. "Cherry Lee, let me hear from you the minute Tom comments on the rooms in that book I let him borrow. Then let's make a date to see the new apartment . . . just for you and me. We'll make another date with Tom to go to a showroom with us and get him fitted for a chair."

She looked puzzled, but the elevator had arrived and I shoved her into it and threw her a parting kiss for comfort.

No matter what the budget, plans, and purchases would be for their starter apartment, Tom would have to be taken out and fitted for a chair.

Fitting a man to his very own chair is one way to get him interested in decorating his home while keeping him comfortable. And quiet. It's a considerate ploy. A man seated in a chair that's been especially purchased because it suits *his* taste and contours is a lot less likely to be a grouch.

I spoke to Cherry Lee's father that evening. He and Minnie

wanted Cherry Lee and Tom to have the best of everything. I would be in charge of purchase and placement. With Milt Simon on the phone and Minnie on the extension, I got double-barreled compliments.

All this meant one thing to me. They wanted the "kids" to live in the lap of luxury—on a tight budget. (On the whole, the more compliments I get on my taste the less money I know is to be spent.) I reminded them that prices had gone up a trifle since they had decorated their home. Not much more than triple, except in most instances.

"Duvie, we trust you completely and we know you'll keep an eye out for bargains." I love being trusted completely. It makes me feel saintly and martyred. Which was exactly what they'd had in mind. One thing had to be straightened out before I marched down the road to heaven.

"Minnie, are you thinking of donating your dining-room buffet to the newlyweds?"

"Well, yes. I'm not really sure it goes with my dining room and Cherry Lee likes it."

"Minnie, it goes with *your* dining room. It's been going with your dining room for about ten years. Besides, it won't fit into the dining area of the new apartment."

Starting out with that lie (because a buffet doesn't necessarily have to be in a dining room), I proceeded. By the end of our conversation, we were all pleased and happy. Even Minnie.

Cherry Lee called me later the same night, whispering, "Guess what Tom's doing? He's reading that decorating book from cover to cover and he's making all sorts of comments. And putting markers on some pages."

Turned out, fortunately, that he wasn't marking up my book or folding down page corners; he was placing paper sheets in the pages that had photographs he liked. And jotting comments on the papers. Not only that, he had called his friends and made an appointment for Cherry Lee and me to see their apartment.

"He wants to know when you want him to meet us at the chair showroom."

We made dates. The apartment first. The showroom second. The book was to be with Tom on the second date. That would give him time to have second thoughts before decision time.

Cherry Lee and I met at the new apartment. We greeted each other in the lobby. The lobby looked like any one of a thousand lobbies. French Prudential with chrome, featuring plastic greenery. Matching doorman.

We arrived at her future apartment doorway via push-button elevator. I was introduced to the present tenant, who was charming, harassed, and about ten months pregnant. Her first comment was "The place is a wreck." That's always the first comment I get when they're told I'm a decorator. Somehow, people seem to think all decorators do postgraduate work at the department of sanitation, neatness division. I could walk through a large garbage heap and coo ecstatically. Or at least keep my mouth shut. An experienced decorator is the last human on earth who would knowingly make any house dweller uncomfortable. (We don't have to, I guess. They already are, just knowing one of us is arriving.)

Would it be better if I were just ushered in as a friend of the family? Absolutely not. To function as the decorator of a new home, I must use my steel tape measure, I must take notes, I must ask for permission to peer into closets, to inspect the bathroom (is the laundry hamper built in? Do we need more storage space?), I must see if curtain rods are already installed and if they will remain (if so, a lot of money can be saved—*if* they're not painted over when the place is redecorated), I must often listen to a sales pitch on the present wall-to-wall carpeting (which may be a good thing for my clients to buy because it's there), I must check on lighting fixtures, and I, too, have to get some feeling about the new space.

Cherry Lee kept poking me. She didn't have to. I can case an area pretty quickly. And this wasn't a pretty area. Here was a very standard apartment done as one would "do" an apartment in order to live in it. All basic living spaces really only require a place to eat and cook, a place to sleep, and a place to attend to personal comforts—a built-in comfort station or bathroom.

What had Tom found so enchanting about the apartment? One, it existed. Two, it had filled the needs of another young couple. Three, it was predominantly beige. The walls were beige, the wall-to-wall carpeting was beige, the draperies were beige. And there were books.

A low bookcase in the entry hall was not only filled, it utilized its top shelf as stacking surface for more books. Since the entry was actually a part of the living room, the theme continued. More bookcases loped, sagged, and generally appeared throughout the living room itself. Some were the wrought-iron put-togethers that look like arthritic hairpins. Others were plain, unfinished wood, mounted on adjustable wall-hung metal brackets.

For seating, there was a slab-type couch—foam rubber covered in nubby brown fabric. Danish modern. That can mean anything from very good to simply awful. A wooden frame supported the two back cushions; the four legs looked like long pencils screwed into the skinny wooden base. No arms.

There were small tables of the same slender breed. These held magazines. Lamps appeared here and there. Mobility in lighting was achieved by the use of extension cords.

The dining area (that should be one word: "DININGAREA," because that's about the size of them) was mostly a table sticking out from the wall, heading for the living room, and taking over part of it. It was surrounded by spindly chairs and covered by papers, pencils, books, and some crackers. Also a candle in a wax-festooned wine bottle. There was a chandelier above the table. Apartment house supplied. A subtle piece of lighting fixture that said, "I will give you lighting without exposed bulbs —if you have sense, you will replace me."

An uncarpeted hall led to an uncarpeted beige bedroom, which housed a bed. Unmade. Mismatched unfinished sets of drawers. A crooked mirror and wedding pictures. *The* most elaborate wedding of all time had joined together these two who now camped out, indoors.

Of course we were offered coffee, which I could hear brewing in the kitchenette. As a matter of fact, I could *see* it; there were no doors separating it from the dining section. (Funny, young couples may live casually but they *do* brew coffee, whereas we so-called perfectionists often serve instant coffee in good cups and saucers. This must mean something. I don't know what. Maybe *we* have some things to learn about—like coffee, for instance.)

As we sipped the very good coffee from plastic mugs, we got the carpet pitch. It was for sale. It had been very expensive. A gift from her mom and dad. The draperies had been purchased ready-made from a department store and were going with them to the new house. The traverse rods that suspended them would go, too? No, they wouldn't fit. Great. We were getting free hardware.

I took a risk and said that we'd buy the carpet if it was cheap. Our hostess named a price and I made negative sounds, plus a few comments about the fact that it costs a lot of money to refit carpeting, it costs a lot to have it removed from the premises, it needed a good cleaning job. Cherry Lee inadvertently closed my comments by saying softly, "I hate the damn thing." The price went way down. (So did Cherry Lee's spirits.)

When we left, I felt I owed an explanation to Cherry Lee.

40

"Here are the facts," I told her. "That carpeting is already there. It *is* good wool, so it'll clean nicely and the gentleman you're about to tramp on it with loves beige!" She took that under advisement.

As we lunched, I told her that the apartment faced south, so it was lighter than she thought. (She had never looked out the windows because she didn't like handling dirty beige draperies.) Then I told her that Tom obviously wanted a place he'd feel free to work in. That books don't necessarily have to flop around wall-to-wall. That bookcases can be handsome *and* movable. (The thought of custom cabinetwork would be a killer to all of us.)

As she struggled with her egg-salad sandwich, I was able to convince her that a beige-lover could be happy with white or pale yellow walls. Because beige is simply a mood color. It is chosen mostly because it is bland. She looked as if she understood, but I really think she was so involved trying to keep that dripping sandwich intact, she would have seemed to approve of anything.

"Is that living room really thirty feet long, like the floor plan says?"

"Yes, if you measure it from the instant you enter the front door. Cherry Lee, forget the measurements—we'll make it *look* big."

"How?"

"By the use of optical illusion."

She was content just to let the whole thing drop and go home. Well, let's just say she wanted to go home. Because she surely wasn't very content.

When *I* got back home, I checked through my folder marked "Ready-Made Sectional Bookcases." They can be had in many finishes, many furniture styles, and many sizes. The heights are pretty standard, but the widths can vary. If you want to be sure you'll be able to rearrange their positioning, simply don't buy very wide ones. Because each is a separate piece of finished furniture, you can place them easily if they're narrow. Buying at least two of them that have closed storage space at their bases is always a good idea.

Those wall units that one installs oneself on tension poles are another story. You get a catalogue that gives you a choice of 1,000 components. You can have fold-down desks, miniature bars for liqueurs, drawer sections, staggered-height shelving, etc., etc. You can also have a complete breakdown. (The assembly alone requires the facility of a graduate architect, and the placement of the individual storage cabinets requires the layout abilities of an artist.)

We could order good-looking sectional bookcases right away and not fall apart over what wall they would go on. We might mass them all together. Or we might separate them. The only thing I *had* to keep together was a couple, Tom and Cherry Lee.

I say that because Cherry Lee was falling apart. She called to say that she *was* a little unhappy over the purchase of the wall-to-wall carpeting. Her unhappiness expressed itself to me in sobs. Tom, who was with her, was unhappy because we hadn't bought the beige draperies.

I talked to Cherry Lee calmly: "We didn't sign a contract to buy the carpeting and we didn't make a down payment or anything. So you can still change your mind. But would you feel better about it if I suggested that we remove the carpeting in the entrance area and also in the dining area? We can use a brass floor molding to finish off the carpet edges, and that will give you just a large rectangle of carpet in the living-room part. Like a rug."

The sound of a Kleenex blowing a nose was heard through the

phone. Then a pause. Then, "Yes, I like that. I'm sorry, Duvie." I told her not to be sorry. But to let me talk to Tom for a minute.

"Tom, the draperies were not for sale. And, really, Cherry Lee didn't like them at all. But we managed to get to keep all the curtain hardware, so we can replace the draperies without *that* added expense. Okay?"

"Oh, well," said Tom, "that's good. But I didn't know Cherry Lee didn't like them. She never told me."

"Tom, what did she tell you was her reason for being so unhappy about the carpeting? . . . I'll ask you questions so you can just answer 'Yes' or 'No.' It was dirty? It wasn't good quality?"

"Yes" was the answer to both questions.

"Tom, she's trying so hard to please you she's forgotten to tell you the truth about how *she* feels."

He stopped me by saying, "Thanks. I'll take care of it. See you day after tomorrow. I'll bring the book, you bring the pretzels!"

When we met at the chair showroom, Tom had the book in one hand and Cherry Lee was holding on to his other hand.

(It was her lunch hour, and he was saying to her that she didn't have to worry about leaving us, because he knew what it was like to always have to rush.) "You know," he said to her, "we've got a lot of time to get our place done—not just a couple of months, a whole lifetime." Then he winked at me and added, "Don't worry, lady, you're not being hired for your perpetual care!"

We ordered his chair in fifteen minutes flat. A modern classic. Molded rosewood with black vinyl "leather" upholstery on a swivel base of chrome. It had a matching footstool with the same style base as the chair. The chair was designed by Charles Eames—elegant in its original form years ago, it will be just as elegant and up-to-the-minute years from now. We bought a copy. (A *good* copy means that the measurements and proportions of the original have not been altered. Mass production and cheaper materials cut the cost.)

Then Cherry Lee left us alone, and we looked at the book. Tom sat on his perfectly fitted chair, I sat on the comfortable footstool.

There weren't many page markers. He liked airiness. He liked a living room with bookcases along the long wall, with space in the middle for a fireplace. He had chosen to make a note on this one. The note said, "Why don't we use desk instead of fireplace? Pictures can be over it same as over mantel thing?"

Another room featured couches that met in a corner. A square table joined them. The corner was all windows, covered in a very sheer fabric.

Then he liked the Port Royal Parlor at Winterthur. A classic Philadelphia formal room transplanted to that famous Delaware museum intact. All gorgeous Chippendale—glowing yellow damasks set against white walls and mahogany furniture. With a crystal chandelier plunk in the middle.

He had marked a page showing a sleek entry hall—beige with lots of gold and red orange. Mostly on small rugs sparkling on wooden floor. Very contemporary.

"Well, now, Tom, it's all very clear. You should have a formal Chippendale room, with modern sofas covered in yellow damask to offset a black leather chair directly under an Irish crystal chandelier. And since we don't have a fireplace, we can build one while we're knocking out a wall in order to have a fully windowed corner."

He knew I was teasing him.

"You were right," he said. "Cherry Lee was in trouble the other night. She wants to make decisions fast, and you know why . . . but she really can't. But mostly she was afraid to tell me. And that's my fault. Sure, I like beige; but I *love* Cherry

Lee. So the reason for this nutty selection of rooms in the book is that we chose them together. Separately."

"Tom, one more thing. Do we buy the beige carpeting and have it cut down?"

"Positively. Cherry Lee told me the whole truth. She doesn't hate beige, just the idea of *everything* beige. The carpet's such a bargain, we both feel it'll give us a chance to get more things we really need and like."

So now I knew that Cherry Lee had chosen the formal rooms. Tom had chosen the contemporary rooms. And now I knew that both of them had chosen each other wisely.

Any home shared by two people should have things in it that each of them likes. No one gives in completely. Each one gives.

There is an odd thing about time. It passes. And so it passed for Tom and Cherry Lee. Enough of it for prenuptial doings, a marriage ceremony, the delivery of some furniture, and the move into their new apartment. (While they had honeymooned, I was working with several painters, workmen, and drapery installers.)

When they returned, the three of us together pushed and pulled furniture, hung some pictures, and plugged in some lamps.

Tom's and Cherry Lee's apartment was not quite done, even after a time lapse of about three months, because furniture is rarely delivered on the date promised. Deliveries are nearly always delayed because of a combination of reasons. The main one is that a piece of furniture comes from a combination of sources. For instance, a chair you order from a showroom in your town is most often manufactured somewhere else. Far away. The fabric that you choose to cover it in is very likely woven far away from the chair factory. By the time your order is processed, the fabric may not be available. While your chair frame stands nude awaiting its covering, the fabric is being woven afresh. In between, the factory that manufactures the finished chair may go on strike or close down completely for a long vacation. They do shut down factories for long vacations. I can't remember what time of the year it is, but it's most often the time of the year when you're in desperate need of a chair.

While all this may be going on, the chair frame itself may not be in stock. Rarely is one frame cut at a time, so you may be standing around waiting for one chair while the factory is waiting for the wood to cut three hundred of them.

After everything gets together and gets done, your chair must be picked up in order to be delivered. This requires a shipper or a trucker, sometimes several, and they haul it to the warehouse nearest you that holds the merchandise for your supplier. Then you're notified that it's in, and must await another trucker's date for delivery to your house. Multiply all this by every item you might order and you can see why I always tell a client *not* to expect prompt deliveries. When they happen —and they sometimes do—rejoice.

The newlyweds' apartment was a place in which to rejoice.

The foyer had become a separate entity. The removal of the entrance carpeting afforded a space that had a highly polished wooden floor surrounding a round rug that looked like a sun, complete with orange rays. A lacquered Parsons table of bright yellow was against the wall opposite the guest closet. It held mail, in an extra wine rack they'd been given. It worked beautifully; its pigeonholes could even hold rolled-up magazines and the daily paper. Also on the table was a handsome wood lamp of modern design with a beige linen shade. Under the table there was a tall wastepaper basket of shiny brass, for holding mail discards—and for umbrellas on rainy days. One of their dining-room chairs—Chippendale, with a seat of honey-and-white patterned linen—made a pretty pattern against the very narrow wall separating the guest closet from the bedroom hall-way.

All the walls were white. That's the choice we'd made. And so were the sheer but very full curtains that attracted one's eye to the far end of the living room. They silhouetted a sleek, long, low sofa that was covered in a buttery-soft fake leather, like melted caramels. It blended with the beige carpeting and had plump extra cushions of bright yellow, dark brown, and tur-quoise, in velveteen. They were filled with down and feathers, so they'd fit a weary head or an aching back.

The bookcases were light wood and covered the long wall. With a space in the middle for a desk. The desk had lots of drawer space and plenty of surface, too. It would never really be cluttered, because we had bought a complete desk set in deep yellow leather. So there were specific places for papers, pencils, pens, and a big blotter. The desk lamp was a copy of a French one: brass with tall white candles holding the bulbs and a round narrow black metal shade. It's called a *bouillotte*. Very classic and elegant, and it gives up to 180 watts of lighting. (three 60-watt bulbs, in this instance).

Above the desk there were different kinds of pictures in dif-ferent kinds of frames. Some were his; some were hers; some were chosen together. About eight of them. We rehung them till they looked right. Holes in the walls? Sure. But I got a jar of leftover paint from the painters, and a can of premixed Spackle to fill up the holes. First came hole, then Spackle, then paint. At the end of the picture-hanging job.

Tom's chair and ottoman were near the couch side of the desk, in front of a bookcase, but it rolled easily anywhere. An-other easy chair was from Cherry Lee's old bedroom. It was fancy French, with a fruitwood frame, a curved back, and two little separate pieces on its wooden arms that were upholstered.

Called a *bergère*. Now it was covered in a silky plaid of bright blue, gold, and brown. It curved out from the shorter wall leading to the dining-area opening. Two low chests of drawers were against that wall. They're called campaign chests and we'd chosen them in a black lacquer finish, with brass fittings. Each one was three feet long; together they covered six feet of wall. These chests can be effective anywhere, and in any type of room.

A white marble lamp with a white silk shade lit up the black top, showing off the modern poster on the wall, and helping Tom to see which piece of audio equipment he wanted to use. On the chests were a tuner, a record player, and a cassette unit. All in simple walnut or black with chrome. The record player had a cover of smoky plexiglass.

Sure, there was stereo. Each speaker was placed on top of a bookcase. One at the far end, the other at the near.

They had decided on a round glass coffee table. It was big but since you could see through it, it wasn't a space killer. On it? Oh, some large colored lacquer bowls, filled with pretzels, mints, or seasonal fruit. Some bright ashtrays for guests. (Cherry Lee had stopped smoking and Tom never had smoked.)

Lighting the couch end of the room was done with one lamp —a marvelous arc of chrome stemming from a heavy marble floor base. The base was on the floor behind the right side of the couch; the lighted milky-white circle at the end of the arc wound up near the left-hand side of the couch. The glow it gave suffused the whole couch and coffee-table section with soft moonlight.

A big, real tree in a tub (bought after much consultation with a plant supplier) threw shadows against the curtains—lit up the white with greenery. Since the curtain wall continued straight into the dining section, the tree acted as a natural divider.

Their dining area was bare of rug and held a round white

The Bewildered Bride-to-Be

modern dining table on a pedestal base. Round is the best for small dining spaces—no corners and, in this case, no legs to hinder closer seating. Their new Chippendale chairs looked lacy around it. Six, all covered in the same honey-and-white linen. So they roamed around easily. One in their entry, as you know, and another as a desk chair for Tom.

Their chandelier hung low over the table. It was polished brass. Large, bold—a nice English reproduction-antique piece. Luxurious lighting.

Since that area was really an extension of the living room, it was draperied in the same white sheer. The wall behind the table was papered in a lustrous gold that looked as if it could have been squares of gold leaf. It caught and reflected light—most impressive from the living room. (Impressive but inexpensive.)

The kitchenette was hidden from view by a simple, ceiling-hung, easy-to-open drapery of woven plastic bamboo. All white. (We had to be very sure it was short enough to clear the floor completely; this type of drapery has a tendency to sag.)

Inside the kitchen? Yellow vinyl-coated paper. Looked like sunshine.

In their bedroom: a very good bed, queen size. An inexpensive room-size rug, in blue and white. It looked Chinese but it wasn't.

The same blue-and-white patterned fabric that they had chosen for bedroom draperies was used for their quilted bedcover. (Quilting keeps wrinkle worries down, and it could be used as a coverlet, too.)

Cherry Lee's old dressing table was now lacquered white and had a good low reading lamp on it; it served as her bedside table and desk. (A matching chair came with it.) On Tom's side was a low chest of drawers in dark wood with a marble top. A taller lamp. The two bedside "tables" didn't match, but their different lamps equaled the same height and had matching black paper shades (an easy way to get the "pair" look).

Tom's tall chest of drawers had doors at the top that enclosed shirt shelves. (The best way to store men's shirts—just as the stores do.) It was placed against a small wall that separated the bedroom door from the long sliding-door closet.

The long wall opposite the bed held Cherry Lee's old dresser, scraped and stained to a dark brown. Fancy French style, of course, now looking grown-up. (Cherry Lee's old girlish bedroom had allowed her to get over the "frill" period. Now she could have a bedroom that wouldn't make a man feel like an interloper or a guest.)

They had almost bought a headboard for their bed that would have cost *much* more than the bed itself. (Which cost plenty, and should.) But I told them that a headboard only serves to keep a bed or a head from knocking against a wall. So we bought dark false-wood paneling instead, and put it on the wall behind the bed, up to the ceiling. It looked very rich. Also very sexy, since it held several large gilt-framed lithographs of Picasso's nudes at play. (Not the signed series, but who needed to look close? The idea came across very clearly. Sex is fun.)

Of course they had a mirror in the room. It was very large, gilded, and looked as if it came out of a Victorian bordello. It was on the wall opposite the bed, running the full length of the bride's old girlhood bureau. They had found and bought it together. It took all of us to put it up, using enough wall plugs and heavyweight picture hooks to hang a Sherman tank.

When they told me their portable color TV was to be installed in the bedroom, I was a little shocked. I didn't say a thing, however, as I'm always having tremors when I'm doing someone else's bedroom. (There's not a question a decorator has to ask about a future bedroom idea that doesn't border on the obscene. Think about it. Just start with "What are your sleeping habits?" And go on from there.)

They had a long brass bench in front of their window. It was covered in red velvet, which looked very dramatic in front of the blue-and-white draperies. For putting clothes or blankets or bedspreads on. Or watching TV shows from. I don't know. But they were mutually delighted with it. And that's what counts.

Their bathroom was almost entirely apartment-house-built-in. Complete to plastic-glass tub enclosure. So their mismatched towels and floor mats looked fine in that white, chrome, and mirrored room. (Everyone had given them towels and wash-cloths in all shades imaginable—but *no* monogrammed ones. Cherry Lee had been firm.)

They lived in the apartment and told me they loved it. I looked at it and thought: They've got plenty of storage space. All mobile. They could rearrange their furniture without ripping out anything. And furniture should be rearranged sometimes. Just because you want to. Or because a room that *looks* marvelous may not work well. And comfort must come first.

Their couch was actually a convertible—it opened to reveal a queen-size bed. (So all their linens and blankets would fit either bed.) They needed extra sleeping space for friends. And, whether they knew it or not, even newlyweds catch colds and need to sleep apart occasionally.

The whole place was easy to maintain. There was no fabric that wasn't washable or dry-cleanable. Even their velveteen couch throw cushions had zip-off covers that could be removed for cleaning.

They'd need extra lighting. But they were still in their romantic lighting era.

The apartment looked as if it cost more than it did. Their dining table and hall table were just plastic copies, which would go easily on a porch someday. Their bookstacks, their campaign chests could all move into a future den (or even his office), but each was so basic in design that it carried no visual price tag.

The only expensive things we'd bought were their dining-room chandelier, the six Chippendale dining chairs (not authentic, but very good), and his leather desk set. Whether they moved to a subdivision or to a mansion, they'd be able to use those chairs with pride, and the chandelier would make any hall a magical place or turn a tiny breakfast nook into something special. A fine leather desk set? Well, it makes a husband think, if *I've* got real leather on my desk, *she* should have real sable on her back. (Or at least real leather?)

3

The Angry-Depressed Recently Divorced

She sat on the edge of an enormous king-size bed, staring at the telephone. If she stared hard enough, it was going to ring and there would be a conversation. Even a wrong number would be welcome. She wanted to hear the sound of her own voice, so that she could be sure she existed.

The phone didn't ring. And there was no one left for her to call. Her friends were away or busy.

She wanted to talk, so she talked to herself.

Carefully, quietly, she said, "No, it's not crazy to talk to yourself. It's crazy not to." Amazed that sound issued from her throat, she rose from the bed and walked around her apartment. A moving job was going on: there were cartons to step over, suitcases to avoid. She touched objects on tables, stroked the edge of a cabinet loaded with piles of dishes and cups. Obviously, there was a lot to be done.

"Well, Madam," she said to herself, "there's sure a lot of work to be done—soooo I think I'll take a bath."

As she immersed herself up to her neck in the hot tub, she noticed that even the medicine-chest door was open, showing gaps on the shelves. A great many bottles and cans were missing.

The Not So Terrible Move

"I've heard that they put real loonies in hot tubs and give them long soaks; this is to relax the brain muscles and makes the nerve ends soggy." With that, she started to sing: "Be kind to your web-footed friends. For a duck may be somebody's mother. They live . . ." She stopped singing and started doing some leg pull-ups. "Above all," she said to the white-tiled room, "I must keep myself beautiful—and not strain my muscles. . . . However, I do not think that white prunes are beautiful." She was looking at her fingers, all crinkled from the hot water.

Out of the tub, she reached for a towel. There wasn't one, so, wrapped in a bath mat, she trailed some puddles to reach the linen closet. After several rolled-up blankets and bedspreads had fallen onto the floor, she found some towels. Hand towels.

Blotting herself dry, she talked her way into another room: "This is not, my dear, what I would call good planning. This is not even what I would call rotten planning. You shouldn't have to *plan* to have one full-size towel."

She was back in her bedroom and found herself seated in the same spot on the big bed. "What I've got to do is face the facts. Number one fact is . . . I must not sit here doing nothing." So she got up, took a small blanket from a nearby chair, went back to bed, and covered herself and went to sleep. The solitary sleeping figure took up just a small part of the large bed. She was a slim section surrounded by bedspread. The very old blanket that exposed her toes and the top of her damp head was one she'd had since she was a young girl.

But she was no longer a young girl. She was a woman. A woman in the process of getting a divorce.

The statistics on divorce in America are staggering, and most recently divorced women (or those who are legally separated) stay in the homes they had when they were married. The husband is the one who moves out. Sometimes because of the

The Angry-Depressed Recently Divorced

children. (Marriages have a tendency to produce children.)

So for the same reason that many miserable couples stay married—namely, for the sake of the offspring—many divorcing couples decide that the wife should stay in the original nest. This way, it is presumed, the young ones won't be any more upset than they already are.

And it *is* better that the wife stays where she is, with or without children. Even women who want a divorce will find that with it comes utter desolation. The business of staying put in agony is infinitely better than moving in agony and having to readjust to a completely new set of surroundings.

Yes, she should be kept busy. But she's usually so darned emotionally exhausted that she can hardly move her body, much less all her belongings.

Her home is going to be a very different place, no matter what. Aside from the fact that all her habit patterns will be changed, there is every possibility that the departing husband will also get to take some of the furniture. This is usually first worked out in lethal conversation by the divorcing couple. From then on, it should be handled by their attorneys. What *you* keep and what *he* gets should be written down and filed with your lawyers.

Because the divorce laws are different in, say, California from what they are in New York, the only valid guide you can have on your way to singledom is your lawyer. In the heat of deciding who gets the cups and who gets the saucers, the divorce lawyer will keep his cool and say something in writing that is little less than oracular in judgment.

It would be ideal, of course, if the divorcing couple decided that they would be intelligent, polite, and sophisticated about the whole thing, but that's often difficult.

So let your lawyers do the fighting.

The Not So Terrible Move

The best thing to do after seeing your lawyer, getting things settled somehow, and finding yourself alone and exhausted is see your doctor.

And that was exactly the thought that occurred to the newly wakened lady we left in the vast bed.

Since most doctors have a lot of patients waiting in their waiting rooms, they don't have the time to listen to the full exposition of emotional problems. But they do listen long enough to give you the right prescriptions, and offer reassurances.

She was told, "Gain five pounds, stop worrying, get some fresh air, and take it easy."

That evening, as she was trying to gain five pounds at dinner, she was joined by her teen-age son, who was overjoyed at the sight of whipped cream and pound cake.

"Listen, Mom," he said, "I'm gonna give an open house."

"My foot you are. This place is a foul wreck."

"Right! But look at it! Half the furniture is moved out, the rest we can throw out. This really is a wide-open house!"

Came the moment of truth. The teen-age boy, who is my son, wanted to get on with the business of living. He expected that his mother could do the same thing for their dismantled home that she did for others. I was his mother and he knew I was having big problems; but all his life he had seen me function as a professional interior decorator.

Now I can look back over my own "terrible move" and tell you how it was done, step by step.

If most recently divorced women can afford it, they should call an interior decorator. Obviously, since I *am* one, I couldn't call in one, but I was going through what I think is the most difficult move of all, the move-in-place. And this time it wasn't just the usual business of taking the same four walls and making them different to change the atmosphere. My whole apartment had to seem new, still had to serve as a family home, *and* had to be my showcase.

But then, isn't every woman's home her showcase?

The first thing I had to do as my own decorator was to get an *objective* point of view, to look at all the familiar territory and see it with completely fresh eyes. Not easy.

Something had to happen that would *force* some fresh ideas. My son helped. Jeff said, "Say, why don't we switch bedrooms?"

I shall now make a flat statement. No matter what, *switch your bedroom.* I don't care if it finds you sleeping in a large closet, the dining room, or an outhouse. The recently demaritalized woman should not sleep in her marital bedroom. Give your ex-husband custody of the marriage bed, the marriage chests of drawers that were his, and all memorabilia of his that were in your "together" bedroom.

Yes, this costs money. But the usual divorcée, who has been through the usual divorce-lawyer routine, has some money. Maybe not a lot, but it's enough to manage on. And this is one time when you've *got* to manage. You're spending money to save what's left of your family, your home, and your sanity.

I moved into Jeff's room. He moved into mine. There were a few brief stops along the way. For one thing, I no longer had the old bed, so I decided to sleep for a *few* nights in our living room. We had a long couch, beautifully slipcovered in French Floral Fantasy (in order to disguise the fact that it was really two separate couches, with sagging bottoms). I woke up for two and a half weeks divided in two separate sections, my bottom sagging.

In my haste to get my own double bed, I had gone to the nearest department store and ordered a box spring, frame, and very firm mattress that was available for immediate delivery. (The words "Immediate Delivery" had kept me away from my decorator-showroom sources, they do not have "Immediate

Delivery" printed on *anything.* But I found out that those same words in a department store are not always dependable, either. "Immediate Delivery" is used for any item that is available on the floor of a warehouse that is located outside of town.)

After assuring the department-store complaint department via telephone that I didn't *care* that the mattress and spring were no longer available in blue-and-white "rites of spring" pattern, that I would stay home on the mornings of alternate Tuesdays to receive the delivery, that I was collapsing from lack of a connected backbone—I got a postcard: "Your order #56897654–21225–785 will be delivered sometime during the day of Oct. 7. Be advised that occupant must be at home to receive delivery."

So the bed parts arrived on a Thursday, sometime after the dinner hour. I received a call on our house telephone advising me that my delivery was in the basement of our building, and that I should come down and get it. I said I would come down in my pajamas and sleep in it. The delivery men said they were not permitted to bring it up. I said, "Bring it up and I will make it worth your while." Thank goodness I had cash in the house.

The bed sections were brought upstairs by three hearty men who wanted to park the whole rig, unassembled, in my entry hall. I made crisp sounds—the sounds of dollar bills being crushed in a hand.

And so the four of us wound up in my new bedroom with my new bed. They put it together in about twenty-two seconds. Then they stopped their herculean efforts long enough to glance around the room. Jeff's posters were still on the walls.

"Lady," said one of the amiable crew, "you sure have a swingin' pad!"

It was with some effort that I got them out. But I finally had my very own double bed. All I had to do was make it up, blind myself to the wall décor, and go to sleep.

The Angry-Depressed Recently Divorced

To make it up, I had to choose between single contour sheets that fit Jeff's bed or what remained of the king-size sheets of my ex-bed. May I suggest that when you order your new bed, order sheets that will fit it and choose your sheet designs with care. It's lovely to sleep between designer sheets with fields of daisies on them. But if the daisies have fallen into disrepair and you find yourself sandwiched between flowers of spring and leopards rampant on a desert gulch, it's not so restful. So be sure you have at least two sets of sheets in white. Or a plain soft color.

My first night's sleep in the smaller bedroom, when I was *finally* in bed, proved something very important. I felt very safe and snug in a small room.

But in the morning I was reminded that it was still a teenager's room. So I carefully removed the posters from the walls and took down the pictures of cars and girls, and the pages out of sports magazines. Then I tried to take down the dark cork on one wall, which had permitted a changing display of ticket stubs, newspaper clippings, and various other mementos dear to the heart of the former tenant. The cork had been purchased inexpensively and applied to the wall with a heavy cement-like glue. If you do not intend to live with cork permanently, do not use a cement that's for permanent installations.

All this galvanic activity led to heaps of junk on the floor, holes in the walls, cork lumps resolutely intact, and the sudden necessity for calling the painters. Since I know professional painters and call them frequently, I reacted with my usual decorator-designed feeling: a well-founded panic brought on by the expected arrival of painters.

This panic is based on sound logic, long experience, and a total recall of stories about *other* people's dealings with painters.

Some prejudiced facts about painters:

The Not So Terrible Move

The boss-painter (sometimes known as a contractor) always comes to size up the job and assure you that he has marvelous new "assistants" and that the job will be done neatly and swiftly. If you hang around the premises constantly, you may see the boss painter on the job for about fifteen minutes. The rest of the time, the "marvelous new assistants" will be grousing, speaking to each other in a newly discovered foreign tongue, and eating sardines with onions in hermetically sealed rooms.

The pricing of paint and papering jobs changes with the humidity.

There is always something wrong with the paint color you have chosen.

The wallpaper you love is either "too cheap" to be hung properly or too expensive to be applied by the regular paperhanger. An expert needs to be called in. He, in turn, will tell you that your walls have a rare tropical disease.

Be firm with the painters. Be a stoic. Just remember someday they will be finished. Here's what you do.

Ask for the price and, after you've recovered, ask for a *written* estimate. Don't call in too many painters for extra bids. You're just postponing the inevitable. The job *will* cost too much and take too long and not be too good, anyhow.

Don't stare at the bare walls when the job is finished. Nobody else is going to notice the streaks and mismatches.

Remove every picture-hanging hook unless you want them painted over and intend to rehang the pictures exactly where they were. Tell the painters you expect all the walls to be "prepared" for painting. This makes you sound informed. It means they're to fill up the nail holes, smooth the plaster, and eventually, *un*paint the doorknobs and keyholes.

Have spare rags around and request *clean* drop cloths. Most times you won't get them, but at least you won't get petrified ones.

Don't forget to keep a jar of cold cream handy, to be used for taking paint off your hands and for fast removal of paint from furniture, mirrors, hardware, et cetera. (It liquefies the paint if applied speedily. Even water-based paint is a chore to remove if it's really dry.)

Wax your good furniture heavily. This will retard the adhesion of paint. Also it will protect the wood from the changes of temperature induced by the constant opening and shutting of windows and doors.

If you're having built-in bookcases painted, use *small* cartons to store the books during the paint job.

If you can possibly avoid it now, *don't* have the insides of your closets done. The closets can be heaped with the book cartons, lamps, shades, pictures, boxes of art objects, *and* you won't have to move your clothes. Painters pile everything into the middle of rooms—then they cover the whole new mountain with their drop cloths. The more you have piled up, the harder it's going to be to get to anything. (Everything you really need is going to be at the bottom of the pile.)

Have the *inside of the closet doors* painted. (This isn't necessary if you have sliding doors.) The closet will *look* completely fresh if the inside of the door swings open and matches the newly painted walls.

Ask about enamel for kitchen walls and other woodwork. Painter will explain in his own inimitable fashion about eggshell finish and high gloss. You smile and say, "I just want to be sure it's really washable, won't chip, and will match the wall paint."

The Not So Terrible Move

Ask what *soft drink* the painters like. Keep it in the refrigerator for them. And try to keep a surface bare in the kitchen for them to eat on!

If you choose wallpaper, ask the wallpaper dealer if it requires a lining or special glue. Get the facts *first;* then you can meet any pitch with straight information.

Tell the painters not to paint your curtain hardware: traverse rods are not usable after they've been painted. If you have wooden poles for café curtains, you might want them painted. However, you'd be better off just washing them.

Remove your Venetian blinds or window shades and have them washed or cleaned while the painting goes on. Except for the bedrooms. You may have to sleep home during the job and you need protection from cold, outside eyes, and the onslaught of the sun at dawn. Take the bedroom Venetian blinds or shades down the day the window frames are to be painted.

Try to spend the nights at a friend's, or at a hotel. (If you stay home, you may suffer slightly from paint odors, from not being able to find your bed, from not being able to use the bathroom, etc., etc.)

Get extra paint in glass jars with screw tops. Label them according to color and whether enamel or flat paint, and store them in a cool place. You'll feel better about the little touch-ups that may arise. (That *will* arise.) There is every possibility that the painters may not come back to do the touching-up you need —until, once again, the whole place needs painting.

"The whole place needs painting"; therein lies the key to getting started on a redecorating project. Nobody, including me, really wants to paint a *whole* place.

As I wandered through my house, I tried to think of themes. I walked barefoot through the living room and several thoughts occurred to me. My emerald-green carpeting was crunchy and crisp underfoot. Close inspection of my toes and the velvet pile of the carpet disclosed the reason. My son's "open houses" consisted of a lot of potato chips being ingested by a lot of kids. It would have to be cleaned (after the paint job).

The vast, sheer white draperies would have to be washed— they were now vast, semi-sheer gray draperies. All told, each thought was really one thought: I wanted a clean, clear, fresh start. The total paint job would be the beginning.

I realized one other thing. Semi-terrifying but, I imagine, true of anyone who must rebuild with what's left of a past: I would have to redecorate the place wall by wall.

Literally, I would decorate only one wall at a time, after the painters had left. By then, each freshly painted wall would be ready for something to happen to it. If I thought of each wall as an individual entity, the whole job wouldn't seem so overwhelming and I wouldn't have to wait for the big idea to happen.

For instance, in that living room with its bright green rug, one whole wall was a splendid mass of built-in bookcases, beautifully constructed in sections, then mounted with moldings.

There the bookcases were, huge, well built—and empty. The books they had been created to hold had gone with their collector. Only about twenty-five volumes of decorating books remained. Should I keep the bookcases and fill them? Go buy more books? Or should I throw out the whole thing? No. Some bookcases were still necessary, especially since one section on the end had enclosed bottom-cabinet space. So I decided that on this particular wall I would make a large central niche by removing about ten feet from the middle of the bookcases. I'd leave the long top shelf (would have to add supports to keep it from sagging) so as to connect the two end sections and make the whole thing seem architecturally intentional.

This meant taking out three bookcase sections, which also

meant I'd have to call a carpenter. But first I decided to call a friend. A friend who constantly complained about her lack of shelf space, because her husband seemed to have joined the Book of the *Week* Club.

We made a deal. She'd pay for the carpenter and the pickup of the disjointed sections in return for the free extra bookcases.

As long as I was expecting the carpenter and throwing things out, I looked around for more things to throw out or rebuild. My eyes glanced at the two-piece living-room sofa. Source of pain, torture, candidate for total overhaul, and a veritable bottomless pit for future investment.

Rebuilding and re-covering a large couch can cost as much as getting a new one.

With the couch out, something else would be gone—the one colorfully patterned fabric in the room that had served to "tie the whole thing together." My room would be untied.

The only large hunk of color that had to stay was my green rug, wall-to-wall in the living room. My nice, carved Louis XV chairs were covered in leather. Two in red leather, one in beige. One of the red chairs was a "lady's chair," little and very graceful. *My* chair. So I decided to put it into my bedroom.

Moving the elegant chair into the inelegant bedroom did a strange thing. It pointed the way to saving some money. I had been staring at Jeff's curtains for several mornings—red corduroy café curtains hung on white wooden poles. I had thought them very boyish. After they were laundered, I also thought them very faded. But with the advent of the pretty red chair, the faded red fabric of the curtaining all of a sudden looked like soft red velvet.

It was then I decided that not only would I do the place one wall at a time, but I would put color in one by one. Just to keep going, I would literally pigeonhole the colors.

For instance, everything red would wind up in my new bedroom. Everything green would wind up in the living room. This is not exactly the greatest design technique in captivity but it was the fastest way to start and keep going.

I took a trip to my dining room and realized it was mostly white, except for the chairs, which were chrome with russet leather. Very modern and skinny and uncomfortable, a magnificently expensive mistake I had made. They stood around a black-topped, chrome-based table and looked very impressive near a mirror on the wall that featured a frame of carved, openwork Balinese wood. The brown lacy-patterned frame had softened the look of the rigid chairs.

My dining-room floor was white—fake travertine marble (vinyl)—and the whole room was lit by a chandelier I have hauled with me for twenty years. Czechoslovakian crystal mounted in feathery bronze—with candles for small flame bulbs—the kind of fantasy that seemed straight out of Tennessee Williams. Gorgeous, valuable, exquisite, but not quite complete and a little askew: a chandelier of ante-bellum decadence.

I color-pigeonholed the dining room. White. With crystal. Following the one-wall-at-a-time rule, I decided that my brown wood-carved frame would get sprayed white. (Doing an intricately carved wooden frame—featuring mostly *holes*—with anything resembling a brush would have been an effort comparable to hand-painting the Eiffel Tower.)

It was with considerable amazement that Jeff heard he was being presented with four ultramodern dining-room chairs. He had so much room in my former bedroom that his furnishings seemed sparse and meager. His modern desk would take one chair and the other three could be scattered around to seat his guests in his own "private apartment." I was glowing with generosity.

Jeff looked at me and said, "I don't want those chairs. They'll be just as uncomfortable in my room as they are in the dining room. Sell 'em. Besides," he added, "when I have company, we'll use the living room."

Then he suggested that I throw out the green living-room carpeting.

I argued. "Jeff, this is my room to entertain my friends and clients in. I'll do it the way I think best. If I do it well, you'll like it, too. You have your own big room now. I need to spread out, too."

My tall son looked down at me and said, "You're the decorator!"

Lean, for a while, on someone close to you; as soon as you can, walk alone. If you *can* walk alone, it's doubtful that you'll ever be lonely.

It was also doubtful that I could entertain anyone past the age of seventeen in my living room, unless they were given to assuming yoga positions. I was reduced to two chairs in that room now.

The ten-foot niche between the remaining bookcases in the living room yawned politely at me. The walls and the bookcases were all white and there is nothing like blank white wall space to look really empty. Also, no color beats white for showing off a silhouette. (The same applies to white clothes; you know how a white dress shows up every figure flaw.)

So I needed a couch with a good shape and lots of pictures to hang above it. The pictures would have to be hung in a fascinating pattern and the bookcases would need to be filled interestingly without too much clutter that might distract from the "magnificence" of the central space.

I sat on the floor and gazed at my first wall.

Then I got up and dug through to the back of one of my closets to find some pictures I had hidden away because I hadn't had wall space for them. (They weren't framed, no client had bought them, and anyway pictures are very personal purchases; these I had chosen because *I* had loved them.)

My taste in pictures runs to line drawings, crisply done watercolors, and original lithographs. One of the lithographs was done in black-and-white with a wash of gray and a large central area of lemon yellow. When the pictures and I returned to the living room, the blaze of lemon yellow became a hunk of sunshine. Against the bold green carpet it almost let out a cheer. There, by sheer accident, was my accent color. My living room would be white, bright green, and yellow. Color happens.

My picture framer hauled out various shades of yellow to mat my pictures. (The "mat" is the large border of paper—or, sometimes, fabric—that outlines the picture itself and is edged by the frame.) Of course, the mat makes the picture larger and makes one think of the cost of the frame itself, which is sold by the inch. So I chose simple frames of wood—in bright gilt, silver, or black. But *all* the pictures would have yellow mats.

I had the whole wall designed in my head as I meandered into my antique dealer. (I try to use one antique dealer at a time, if at all possible, because this gives him more business and gives me more bargaining power.) One should always "meander" into an antique shop. This shows that you're uninterested, broke, and just looking for a place to relax. Naturally the dealer is totally unimpressed by the entire acting job, but it makes you feel like a wise shopper.

One thing does impress an antique dealer, aside from the fact that you've been a steady customer, and that is CASH. Like everyone else, antique dealers get very little cash, and it can help you get a better buy, because *they* can get better buys using that cash to pay for *their* purchases.

I was looking for a couch with a splendid silhouette. Something with a grandly carved wood frame, airy in feeling, curvy, with graceful legs that would let it "float" on the green carpet as it assumed its rightful position on my niche wall. Price was no object as long as it was cheap.

"What are you lookin' for, Duvie?"

"A lamp." (Everybody knows you never tell the antique dealer what you're looking for, because he'll automatically raise the price; you just accidentally stumble over what you really want and take him by surprise. In other words, *everybody* is wrong. Nothing surprises an antique dealer more than the whole truth.)

"You know I don't have any lamps—"

"I know, but I thought you might have a couch I could make into a lamp."

"So look around."

And I had been doing just that. If you're looking for something that you have designed in your head—be it a couch or a corset—you're never going to be able to find it. It's purely idiotic to think so. (How many times have you decided you wanted a basic black dress and bought a red, green, and purple print? *All* the time. Unless, of course, you *want* a red, green, and purple print; then you're bound to come home with a basic black.)

Why, then, did he have a couch that was exactly what I wanted? I think I know why. I was looking for a fancy couch when, it would seem, the whole world was looking for a simple couch. If you stay away from the fads of the moment, you're a lot more likely to be able to fulfill your fantasies.

The dream couch not only had a dark hand-carved frame all loopy and swooping, but it had open arms and enough graceful legs to float a centipede. It was about seven feet long and upholstered in pink-and-white silk. The fabric had been popular in a more sumptuous era and, obviously, greatly appreciated; only extensive use could have made it into the shredded wheat it now was. The innerspring construction was now outerspring construction.

When I sat on it, I was almost engulfed by feathers and coils and webbing. I coolly appraised the structure by stroking the framework, by peering underneath to see the springs that stuck out of the bottom, by jiggling the arms to see if they were loose, and after reassuring myself that everything was wrong with it I said, "I've *got* to have this couch or I'll die right here on it."

How's that for putting yourself into a real bargaining position? My antique dealer had me exactly where he would want any customer to be. At his mercy.

"Duvie, what client is going to spend all the money it's going to take to put that thing into shape?"

"Me . . . it's for me."

He reaffirmed my faith in antique dealers. He did not tell me it had been used only on Sundays by a little old lady who had sat on it before going to church. He did not tell me it was an authentic anything. We both knew it was not new, but neither of us knew how old it *was*, either. All he said was that he didn't see any nails in its construction (a good omen—means wooden dowels were used, which is a sign of old craftsmanship), but we both agreed that it could use a few nails, plus screws, bolts, rivets, and concrete cement.

He named a price. I accepted and insisted that he take payment immediately, in cash. His price was fair, but, more important, I bought the couch I loved—and made my antique dealer love me a little more. Always buy the thing you fall in love with, even if you don't need it or it's all cockeyed. If you don't, you'll spend the rest of your life regretting it, while it grows more beautiful and unattainable in your dreams.

I called my old friend the upholsterer to say I had purchased a lovely wooden frame that needed some work—and some upholstering. (Always have your upholsterer pick up the piece of furniture you have bought; that way he takes care of the trucking and you feel as if the piece were being transported at no charge. That's not true; the cost is tucked away somewhere in the upholsterer's bill, but you feel better about its being hidden from view. Anyway, the price usually runs less than would the cost of a private trucker.)

The upholsterer called me back a day later and said he'd picked up the couch. "That's a beautiful frame, Duvie . . . needs a lot of work, though. What are you covering it with?"

I had given absolutely no thought to the fabric that would be needed so that the rebuilt item could function as an actual couch. Not just as a frame silhouetted against a white wall. But the last thought—"frame silhouetted against a white wall"— forced words into my mouth.

"I want to cover it in white, so the frame really shows up, and I want lots of antique-finished brass nailheads *close together*. See, I want that dark wood frame to really show up."

"Nailheads? You covering it in leather?"

"Well, uh, yes. Not real, though. I'll get some soft, grainy leatherette. Be more practical and a lot cheaper."

Suddenly I had remembered that upholsterers think rich. Especially when they're talking to decorators.

Upholsterers see antique furniture purchased by decorators and think of the rich clients who will be receiving them.

"Say," I said, "I think you'd better know that couch is for my own personal living room, and I've got a chair that needs redoing, and who knows what else. And I'm calling all my old clients and telling *them* to have everything redone." (*You* could say the same kind of thing just by changing the word "clients" to friends. It's still the same functional lie.)

"Duvie, I hope you got that frame as a gift, because it's going to cost a bundle to fix it."

So I offered to pay *him* in cash, too. This is attractive to anyone. Except in the case of the upholsterer—he's paying his workmen and the price of labor isn't going down for him or me or you. And he's not going to pay *his* help in cash. (He'll use it to buy antique furniture frames to sell to decorators.)

Only the promise of more work helps cut the cost of upholstery. So I quickly told him to get to my house to pick up my chair and whatever else I could find. Sometimes more is cheaper.

Your upholsterer is the man who will tell you the exact yardage you need to cover a piece of furniture.

Fabrics come in different widths. A 36-inch-wide piece of material may seem a lot cheaper to you than one that is 54 inches wide. But by the time it has been joined together in the right way, you may wind up spending more because you *need* more. Large-scale prints require larger-scale purchases, too, because the pattern is "repeated" at various intervals—and if it isn't repeated well it'll mean you can't ever turn over a couch cushion. Just think of big sunflowers with leaves. Each clump of sunflower and leaves is one repeat. If you're stingy about your chintz, you're going to have a couch that looks terrible. There can be a lot of waste in most fabric used by a good upholsterer, but it's honest waste.

I had requested nailheads "close together." Nailheads are most often used to apply leather to a wooden frame. Close-together nailheads are a sign of good workmanship. They serve as a smooth outline and don't distract from the shape of the frame. (Fabric can be applied without nails showing; this is done with spaghetti-like piping covered in the same upholstery fabric and glued or stitched over the hidden nails.) There are many variations on upholstery and slipcover techniques; a good upholsterer knows what's best. Don't hope to save your money on this kind of labor.

As I accomplished more in the house, it got emptier. What

hadn't been traded away had been given away. I gave the dining-room table and chairs and the old couch to a charity. They give you a tax deduction. I didn't *need* a tax deduction but, more important, I didn't need that furniture and I didn't want "shoppers" coming to my house. If those things had been valuable antiques, I would have tried to sell them. But advertising furnishings for sale can lead to lots of strangers coming in, and if you're not dead-broke, keep unknowns out of your house. You'll be safer, and will avoid feeling poverty-stricken.

The important thing was that I knew the place was going to take shape. Knowing your orders are in and your excesses are out is a fine feeling. It's a kind of neatness of the head.

My heady neatness led me to a new habit: I made up my bed the minute I got up in the morning. There is nothing like an unmade bed to make a woman feel that she's not managing her house. A certain kind of obvious orderliness makes you feel as if your life isn't in total disorder.

My white bedroom had become the place for the "reds." But I didn't want a red bedspread, so I just took two color steps down from red and got to pink. A pale pink quilted bedspread covered my new white sheets. But nothing covered the polished-wood floor.

I like rugs in a bedroom. But not "scatter" ones. I think they're dangerous in a room where you're often staggering around in the dark. Even if they don't slide because they're well anchored, you're liable to trip over an edge. A big, soft rug in a bedroom is safe and practical.

I bought my rug from my usual carpet store. I did *not order it;* I walked in and said I wouldn't buy anything unless I saw what I liked and could have the *same one.* So I got an ivory, red, and pink room-size rug. A room-size rug usually means anything from a 6 × 9 to a 9 × 12, unless you're going for custom-made or you live in a teacup. We live in an age of rugs and carpets and floor coverings. Price and quality change from store to store. Ask questions, watch the newspaper ads, buy what you like, and don't spend a lot of money on a bedroom rug. You don't need the rug that the salesman says, "will last the rest of your life." It won't; it shouldn't have to; you'll get tired of it; and why worry yourself to death about taking care of it?

My red, white, and pink bedroom became complete, one wall at a time, too. I wakened in the morning to see the wall in front of me achingly empty. That was solved by bringing in a small English flat-top desk. I put on it a ruby glass lamp with a white shade and, on the wall above it, an old mirror and a charming picture of Jeff when he was little.

Be sure the wall opposite your bed holds something you love. Forget the rules: hang old pictures of family or friends, or use a bookcase filled with the books you've read with joy; just be sure that when you open your eyes, the wall you see says, "Good morning."

My red leather lady's chair fit with the flat-top desk as well as the miniature oak roll-top desk that I type on—I had cornered this little work desk with its myriad drawers so that I could get window light.

My "bedside tables" were not bedside tables. One side of the bed held my black-and-white file cabinet. On the other side, nearest the entrance, my phone and date books, ashtray, and white marble reading lamp, with its black paper shade, were all on a large, low, round white marble-topped table. It had plenty of surface for all the things that make for nighttime comfort.

That functional file cabinet brought my bedroom accent color into being. It needed something on top of it that would keep it from looking businesslike. I have a huge Bristol blue bowl with a pitcher, the color of a brilliant summer sky. When it landed on top of the cabinet, I knew that this sparkling blue was the "extra" I needed. Funny thing, I've collected blue china and glass for years, and I'd kept it in a closed cabinet that had been opened only for company. Now my best pieces from my best collection would keep *me* company. Everything in your most intimate room should be what you value most intimately. It makes *you* feel valuable.

Of course I had a chest of drawers for my clothes and a many-tiered magazine rack, and closets. (And someday I'd get around to straightening them out.) All storage space was used as temporary storage. Neatness in those areas doesn't count at all, sometimes. You can't possibly cover every area when you're pulling yourself together.

My couch came back and looked as if it had been made for that special living-room wall. Which it had. And the yellow matted pictures spaced themselves above it with no ease whatsoever. They took me four and a half hours to hang and rehang, until they looked exactly right to my eye. Hanging pictures consists of rehanging pictures. The *only* rule is to have that extra Spackle to fill the nail holes and extra paint to retouch with.

The books didn't fill enough of the bookcases, so I faced many of the bigger ones frontward. Too much galloping color exploded from some of the book jackets. I removed the jackets and stored them away. The books looked calmer.

We looked at our living-room wall and saw thirty feet of utter elegance. We sat on our white couch and saw stars! Not just from the glass coffee table in front of it, which seemed to have become a multifaceted emerald—with its green crystal box and more crystal objects glittering over the green rug—but from the fact that the couch was made to *look* at, not to sit on. I felt as if I were sitting bolt upright waiting for an ambassador to arrive.

And that's how another wall got decorated. I bought a white wicker day bed with deep back cushions and a mattress seat. All

74

covered in a fabric of cotton featuring face-front daisies. Big, happy daisies on a black field connected by green leaves. The most informal, comfortable piece of furniture imaginable. And extra sleeping space for a guest or for smaller quarters that I might easily move to in a couple of years. The necessity for comfort can lead to interior decorating.

I walked around with lamps and small tables until the room was evenly lit. Then I switched lampshades or bought new ones, ready-made. Lampshades are the biggest tip-off to a newly done house. The shapes of shades change from year to year—look around the stores and you'll see. One year, tall slender shades; another year, pleated plastic shades that flare; next year, perhaps, low drum shapes. (Sure, I bought one bright yellow paper shade.) Then I put in the right-size light bulbs. *At night.* Because that's the time you see if your lighting works, with smoothness, softness—or brilliance, if you wish.

A living-room cabinet switched places with an entry-hall cabinet. With that, the entire look of the entrance hall changed (and another living-room wall got done). The entry hall's new cabinet had been the one that housed my blue collection. I opened the doors of it permanently and, presto, the entry hall became blue and white. The chandelier changed its looks because I put little blue lampshades on it. Then the hall chairs got blue seats.

Connecting the separately done walls in the living room was achieved by placing chairs at angles, by covering a round table to the floor in a bright green felt, by putting a round glass vase full of tall leaves in a corner. Each corner was rounded as I got to it.

Any well-done living room has "tribal" seating. In other words, you *sit* in a circle. Unless the room is so vast that you have separate seating areas. But, even then, I'll bet you'll find people sitting around in tight little circles within each area.

The Not So Terrible Move

"Well," said Jeff as our new white wrought-iron-and-glass dining-room table and chairs arrived, "isn't it time *you* gave an open house?"

Seventeen friends arrived for what I announced as a "trim-the-tree" party. It seemed fitting to me because it was Christmastime; they figured I'd do anything to get presents. Nobody knew I was testing out my new house for reactions—except me. And I had enough paranoia and pretzels to serve everyone.

It was the noisiest party I've ever had. But this is what I heard from an old friend talking to his wife: "Sitting in this living room is like being inside a ginger-ale bottle—all yellow and green and white. It bubbles!"

I wondered if I'd be happier if he'd said champagne. No, champagne is for special occasions; ginger ale is a comfortable, everyday refreshment.

A former client, now a friend, came over to me and whispered, "Duvie, you finally got what you've always wanted—a summer house!"

It was true, and I hadn't even realized it.

So I had a year-round summer house in town, eleven stories above a city street. I invited my friends "up" instead of "out," and soon noticed that lots of new faces came to visit.

4

The Utterly Lost Widow

I am very pleased to tell you that there is a life after death.

And how I know about it is that a very lovely lady named Cecily proved it to me. She ought to know. You see, a while ago she lost her husband, Mat, and with him she felt she'd lost everything. They had been together a long time and had become so interlaced they reacted and acted as one person. When he'd died, she thought she'd lost not only him but herself.

Here is the story of how she became alive again.

And it all begins with a lampshade.

When I had first done their apartment many years ago, I had found a spectacularly beautiful black lamp made from an old Chinese vase. When I had put it in place on one of their French tables, her husband said to me, "I think it would look more impressive if it had a lampshade on it."

True enough. Even very expensive antique lamps look weird with just a light bulb showing. I assured him, "I have the perfect shade in mind for that lamp. Wait till you see it."

Meanwhile, I pulled an old lampshade out of one of their closets and put it on the black lamp temporarily. If you have the room, always save a couple of old lampshades. That way you'll always have something to shield your eyes from light bulbs

The Not So Terrible Move

while awaiting the arrival of the new lampshade. (Lampshades wear out faster than lamps, remember.)

When I had said, "Wait till you see it," they had reacted simultaneously. They had grown used to waiting, because almost everything they had was custom-made. And that certainly means waiting.

Purchasing or designing the right lampshade requires great skill, artistic intuition, measurements and other statistics, and a lot of luck. As a matter of fact, forget everything else and just depend on luck. Unless you wish to haul a huge lamp around with you and keep trying shades on it.

Most times, I go to the lampshade department of a store, buy lots of shades that are returnable, then take them back to the shadeless lamp (or lamps) and see which looks right. The wrong ones I return to the store, tags and cellophane or plastic covers still intact, and get a refund. Which is better than getting a dislocated shoulder. (By the way, the shade that's finally found a lamp to fit it has its cellophane or plastic cover immediately removed. Those transparent covers only serve to slowly warp the shade when it's lit. Like sleazy emergency plastic rainwear, they're hot inside, induce interior moisture, and look miserable.)

But this black lamp was so handsome I decided I'd better have a shade custom-made. On my way to the lampshade makers' I found a question was on my mind. What kind of shade *would* be right for that lamp?

I had the correct measurements with me and I looked around the premises for an idea. Wire frames hung from the ceiling, odd-shaped shades in odder colors awaited pickup—and *one* lampshade stood askew on what seemed to be a pregnant dragon.

That shade was simple, very large, superbly hand sewn, and perfect for the topless black lamp. (It had been ordered by a decorator who had never come back to get it and whose phone had been disconnected.) I could have it for a great deal of money. And I could not bring it back for a refund.

Finding the right thing immediately is a stroke of luck I've had several times in my career. I always mention this because I try to forget the 4,563 times things have gone wrong.

Anyway, I took the lampshade to the lamp and it was fine for it. The shock of the fast delivery almost relieved the shock of the vast price, and I think that lamp and shade became the most treasured item in their house.

It was through a chance meeting many years later with one of their friends that I heard of Mat's illness.

I intended to call Cecily but I waited too long. And then *I* heard from *her*. Mat was just out of the hospital and she needed a rocking chair for him. He could sit up for short spells, and a rocker would be comfortable and not too orthopedic-looking, she thought.

I began searching for one and the rocker was delivered about a week later, with me accompanying it, and was a success.

The last time I saw Mat, he was sitting in his new rocker, telling Cecily she ought to get out of the house and get her hair done. As she saw me to the door, I heard him call to me: "Duvie, found any cheap lampshades recently?"

Not long after that, I was at their home again. It was crowded with people. The food was lavish, the silver shone, the lamps were lit, flowers were everywhere, Cecily was serving her guests. But Cecily was in black.

Surrounded by her friends and family, it was as if Mat would walk in momentarily and say he was glad she'd had her hair done.

A lot has been said about the barbaric customs of funerals and the gatherings after them. But the only insulation against overwhelming despair is people. Whether Cecily knew it or not, she was exhausting herself even further by her constant attendance upon her guests. But wisely her family let her do it. Physical tiredness would aid her now.

Hearing from Cecily three months later came as no surprise to me. (I'd called her a couple of times and been told of the kids finally going back home and of the sister who stayed with her for a while.) I'd *expected* the call that would say "I want to move. Come, let's talk."

Most widows want to move. Most move too fast. Far too often, houses and possessions have been sold quickly and at great loss. Not only is the loss financial, but the moving away pulls up roots that are deep and necessary. You can't move away from sadness. I've watched it: sadness moves away itself, and then only with time. Grief can be compounded and extended by making a fast move and regretting it later.

I went to meet Cecily at her apartment and I went armed to the teeth with *facts.*

If she could afford it, she should stay where she was.

She should rearrange her furniture, not her living habits.

I knew that though Cecily's apartment was large, it was not too large to live in alone.

Since I had worked as their decorator for years, I was aware of the fact that they had supervised their money handling together. She would not be one of the large group of recently widowed women who find themselves without funds because of the harrowing technicalities of wills, tax laws, locked vaults, closed checking accounts, complicated insurance policies, or unrealistic trust funds. Rich wives have often become poor widows because of their not being aware of the financial facts of life —or, just as important, of death.

When Cecily opened her door for me, I was delighted to see her wearing a long colorful robe. She looked weary but well, hair and nails done; she moved around the living room swiftly, turning on lamps, adjusting ashtrays, and generally being a hostess.

"You know, Duvie, I've been alone here now for almost two months and I don't mind it at all."

"Well, then, why do you want to move?"

"Oh, the place is too large, really . . . and I want to travel and . . ."

"Cecily, this place is *not* too large!"

"I want to be able to come and go as I please. Take trips and come home to a—to a place where I can just keep a few things, and not have to worry. . . ." And her voice trailed off as her eyes looked around the room.

So did mine. I had been intent on her and what she was saying. Now I looked. Everything was in place. The paintings were lovely, the furniture was superb—two Louis XV chairs covered in petit point were vivid from the light cast by the black Chinese lamp.

I automatically walked over to inspect our treasured lamp-shade. As always, I reached out to correct its nonexistent tilt. Then I saw what I had never seen in her home before. There were cobwebs on the lampshade.

The room was dead. Because no one had been living in it. Cecily may have been taking care of herself, but there was not enough care left over for the objects she had loved.

On the pretense that I wanted some water with ice, I went to the kitchen and its refrigerator. There was no fresh food in it. Only old jars of pickled things or jellies. In the freezer, with the ice-cube trays, were a few boxes of frozen vegetables, their packaging discolored from age.

Back in the living room, as I sipped the strange-tasting water (old ice cubes have a taste I can only describe as rotten), I wondered how I would tell her she had to move.

"Duvie," she said, "I haven't been in this room since my sister left. I sit in the bedroom in Mat's rocker. It's as though I'm waiting for something to happen or someone to come in. I'm not afraid. I'm just utterly . . . lost."

A house is worth keeping only for the people in it. The mere act of housekeeping itself would have proved Cecily should stay where she was and change the looks of the house around her. She had, in effect, already moved out.

"Okay, Cecily, you're going to find something soon. You've got to find an apartment you like, and then we've got to make plans for packing and moving. So I'd suggest you start eating some thawed food, taking vitamins, and getting the newspapers late at night or early in the morning." First one at the classified-rent ads gets first crack at the good apartments.

Her relief was a joy to see. She cried. People, like foods, weep when defrosting.

The next set of joys was watching Cecily, the heretofore perfect housekeeper, become Cecily, the perfect house hunter. She not only bought every newspaper, she called and alerted every friend. Then she made her biggest decision. She would move—but not out of the neighborhood. The shops, the storekeepers, the general atmosphere of the area had made her happy. So she limited her looking to a specific section. Her own.

She called to tell me there was a place to look at. So we looked at it—and it was awful. Not only was the apartment all chopped up architecturally (too many doors for too few closets and everything on a tiny space scale), but the sounds in the hall during the day proved it would be mayhem at night. Loud music, babies crying—the telling symptoms of the wrong building. We both realized it.

Next time out, we found it. No, it wasn't a gorgeous place, but it had the feel of home. From the entrance on the street, through the lobby, up the elevator, and into the hall to her future front door, the building was in her category. Any apartment can be fixed up, but no amount of fixing will fit you into a building that is either too young or too old for you. If the tenants are swinging singles and young marrieds, you'll be old before your time from sleepless nights. If the building has too old a feeling, enfeebled tenants, too aristocratic a lobby, doddering doormen, you'll be just as uncomfortable. Your apartment must be, sort of, the filling in a happy sandwich. The right building is the right bread.

Cecily had found three rooms. Available immediately, which meant she had to pay rent on two places at once. Her landlord at the old apartment was notified of her intention of moving at the end of the month. All the ramifications of getting out of the old lease and into a new one were put in the hands of her lawyer. Then she moved into the stage of spending money on unseen items.

Whether you're moving across the country or across the street, you've got to do the same packing. If the move is a short haul, you may do some of it by hand, by car, or whatever other aid you come up with. But moving is not a do-it-yourself job.

First, you should decide what you're going to take, which means you've supposedly decided what you're *not* going to take. Then you inform the movers of what they're to haul to the new address. Get hold of the movers the minute you decide on where you're going. Somehow, moves are always projected to take place on days when everyone else is moving. Or on a national holiday. Or when there's a snowstorm. Or a flood. You can't do a thing about an act of God, but you can control elevator flow. (Will the two buildings have an elevator available for your move out and in?) Good movers can handle *almost* the whole job, but the basic plans are up to you.

I convinced Cecily to hire the best movers. She could save a little money by packing some things herself. Good movers will supply the right cartons and barrels, cardboard clothes closets, and do crating—before the deadline. But unless you've got the physique of a wrestler and the stamina that goes with it, forget about saving money on moving. Moving costs a fortune, but it's worth it if you save just one pulled muscle. And I'm not even thinking about breakage. (Good movers are insured. Your broken furnishings will be fixed or replaced. It's not so easy to fix a broken body.)

All we had to do then was to decide what she was going to take. And as I said, that comes only after one has decided what one is *not* going to take. There were two of us to make those decisions, but basically the decisions had to be hers. We walked around her five-room apartment; she talked to herself and I listened.

"Can't bear to get rid of that."

"The kids may want that later."

"My Lord, Mat and I bought that the day after we were married."

The only things she was sure she didn't want to take were the refrigerator and stove, which belonged to the building. And so we decided we'd move everything into the new apartment and get rid of the excesses later. No, it wasn't sensible to move five rooms of furnishings into three rooms of fresh paint. But this was one of those times when it was best to let sentiment take precedence over common sense.

When it came to removing the wall-to-wall carpeting she had in almost every room in the old place, I told her to reconsider. Removing, cutting, cleaning and reinstalling carpeting is not only expensive but it binds you to color and inhibits the shoving around of furniture that has to take place. In other words, if you don't have to, don't haul old carpeting with you. We hoped that the future tenants of her apartment would buy it. If they didn't buy it from her, I suggested she tip her present superintendent by giving *him* the carpeting (and the responsibility for having it removed).

Don't forget to tip your old superintendent as well as your new one. It will make moving day easier. (Also, your lighting fixtures will be removed and reinstalled with promptness and smiles. To say nothing of the fact that you may get new window blinds or a new stove. And nobody will complain if you take a favorite shower-head fixture with you.)

Awaiting moving day, Cecily was washing her china, polishing her silver, and waxing all her furniture. That way, when it was unpacked, everything would be clean and ready to use. (Waxing the furniture cuts down on some of the scratches that inevitably happen.)

I checked on the paint job in the new apartment. Empty apartments paint fast. Also lousy. Unless someone checks during the time the painters are in action.

She wasn't getting a "custom paint job." She was getting an apartment-house-supplied paint job. That meant tip first, pray later. The apartment-house-supplied paint is usually something resembling diluted milk of magnesia. The color-range choice goes from off-white (which we chose), through bleak, to drab. By dint of giving extra money, I managed to get *all the wallpaper* removed from the bathroom walls; enamel over scrap paper is an effect that should be avoided.

I saw that the light switches were not painted into stationary position. I got the now friendlier painters to scrape off the chipped, hard paint on the built-in air-conditioning/heating units, so that the fresh paint went on smoothly. They painted the insides of the kitchen cabinets. (The outsides were Formica, so would scrub clean.) The light plugs were kept from being filled up with paint. (Because I covered the little socket holders with masking tape—they wouldn't look so great, but they'd be covered by a plug anyhow, and no one would get shocked or frustrated trying to jam them open later.)

Moving day went as always. Organized chaos. About the move out of the old apartment, Cecily said, "It's going so fast I can hardly believe it." As we walked away from the soon-to-depart van, I told her, *"Don't* believe it." Because that healthy-looking van would possibly have a breakdown, there would be the world's longest lunch hour (movers do not *eat,* they *dine*), and somehow the new building always has a malfunctioning elevator—the one that's been reserved for *you.*

So while we were sitting on the floor of the new apartment waiting for the movers to arrive, Cecily said, "Shouldn't we have had these floors redone? They've got paint blotches—and look at the scratches!"

I cheered her up by telling her that floors should be left bare and miserable-looking until all the furniture had been hauled in and around and finally found the right spot to stay. (Sometimes just a good heavy cleaning and waxing does the job, especially when you know rugs will cover a lot of the place, too. Why redo a whole floor when only a few sections may need doing?)

Then she checked on some of the things she had brought over by hand: small cartons of art objects, a large painting she didn't want to have crated, and lamps with shades. In the middle of the bare floor was the black Chinese lamp with its shade tilted. She carefully straightened the shade. We looked at each other and laughed.

The movers entered while we were laughing. Good sign. For the next couple of hours, we didn't have time even to snicker, sneeze, or breathe consistently. The movers kept asking, "Where do you want this, lady?" Since we had a wide choice of living room, entry hall, or bedroom, we kept saying, "Oh, just put it anywhere." Except for big things like couches and beds. And *they* looked bigger than ever.

The Utterly Lost Widow

The movers exited at dusk. While we were once again laughing. Because Cecily was determined to find the carpet attachment for her vacuum cleaner, and I'd reminded her that the only carpets she had now were bath mats.

By the time I left, she had made her bed. The linens and blankets from it had been neatly folded, put into a pillowcase, and set on the exposed mattress. They *were* good movers.

And, yes, the new superintendent had seen to it that a handyman was available to do little things like reassemble the beds. (No, the movers don't have to do that, and with their hourly charge you'd have to be a looney to request it.) Best of all, the handyman would reappear in the morning to start helping us shuffle furniture.

When I sank into my bed, I was sure Cecily must be sound asleep or, at least, unconscious in her new house.

Then she phoned me to ask if I was awake. It seemed to me that maybe an hour had passed. No, it was 10:00 A.M., and she'd been up since six after having retired at three.

First thought: She was overdoing it.

Second thought: Oh, no, she wasn't. She was being Cecily, housekeeper. She was home again.

I managed to semi-crawl over by eleven-thirty, and she greeted me at the door with a cup of coffee.

"Well, how do you like it?" she asked.

"Huh?" (Honestly, what was there to like in an apartment that had an acre of furniture shoved into what seemed like a shoe box?)

"Oh, I don't mean this," she said, with her arms waving around the piles, mounds, crates, and cushions, "I mean *this!*" And she opened the guest closet door. The hangers were neatly lined up. Several small matching closet bags were already in place. Her hatstands marched across the top shelf.

From there she guided me into the kitchen. Her basic dishes

were in place in the cabinets. Her kitchen silverware was neatly arrayed in a separator box in a freshly paper-lined drawer. The cleaning supplies were stored away in a cabinet under the sink. Her mops, brooms, etc., were standing at attention in the broom closet.

"Look." She opened the refrigerator. Glistening, it held fresh milk, orange juice, eggs in the egg tray, bacon, little cheese-boxes, new glass containers of edibles. There were fruits in the fruit bin, freshly washed lettuce in the vegetable section.

She must have gone shopping shortly after dawn. What could I say? I was overwhelmed, yet *I* was too tired to give her enthusiastic applause.

"All I want to know, Cecily, is . . . did you find the carpet-cleaner attachment?"

Yes, but she couldn't seem to locate the bath mats.

It would have been easier to get around the house wearing stilts, because of the closely packed furniture, but we continued our tour of closets and medicine chests. She had done all her hidden interiors. She was actually asking me if I could order shelf borders and window shades, which I sometimes use to conceal sections of closet storage areas.

"Cecily, I can even order fresh flowers for your dining table, but at the moment I don't think I can find the table! Don't you think we ought to start sorting out this warehouse?"

She tentatively sat down in the rocking chair, which was propped up tightly against a love seat. The love seat was almost directly connected to one of the twin beds. She looked around the jammed bedroom, and very, very softly she asked, "Where do we start?"

Somehow she seemed very small. She was holding on to the chair arms tightly. Holding on for dear life. She had made her terrible move—but now she could move no farther. I had to keep her busily involved with the hundreds of details that would help her feel she was accomplishing something. Instead of staying inside herself, she was staying inside closets, cupboards—so the next step?

"Cecily, why don't you start straightening your dresser drawers? Dresser drawers always get tilted during a moving job. So straighten them out."

Then she would discover she no longer needed so many chests of drawers. Her neatness would impel her to get rid of one extra chest soon.

As she started on her assigned job, I got the handyman into the bedroom. NEVER SHOVE FURNITURE ALONE. Beg, borrow, or steal someone with a strong back and a dolly, which is one of those flat wooden platforms on wheels that professional movers use.

Immediately, we separated the twin beds and put *one* night table between them. This meant we wouldn't need the original two and the pathway between the beds afforded a stretch of open floor space that fooled the eye into believing there was more room than there really was.

The long dresser Cecily was working on slid into position on the wall opposite the beds. Now all we had left was an extra night table, Mat's tall chest-on-chest, his rocker, a love seat, and two upholstered French armchairs. All we *needed* was ten more feet of bedroom.

"Let's move the love seat into the living room where it can join all its friends," I said to Cecily and the bewildered handyman.

In order to move anything anywhere in the living room, we had to get rid of the cartons. In order to do that, Cecily had to unpack them. So we had them put in one section of the entry hall and she was kept busy.

I directed the handyman. The dining table was located under a pile of sofa cushions and book boxes (and a box of bath mats).

The Not So Terrible Move

Emptied, the table stretched across one *whole* end of the living room near the kitchen door. Its eight chairs fenced it.

I used an old theory. Case pieces against the walls. Those are all large wooden pieces, like breakfronts, bookcases, carved chests. Upholstered pieces in island-type sections in the room middle.

So the big couch separated the dining section from the living-room part. Not directly centered, so that it could get some light from a chest on the wall near it. Its coffee table was placed off-center, too.

The love seat was angled with a small flat-top desk behind it. On either side of the large handsome bookcase, two chairs faced into room center. (One was Mat's brocade-covered wing chair. All I wished was that wing chairs could fly. It was a beauty but its size was in the condor division.)

I used the window wall as if it had draperies—in other words, as if it were a solidly covered stretch of wall space. A long refectory table was placed in front of it, and in front of *that* the old couch from the old den. A pair of lamps went on each end of the table backing and lighting the couch. A whole lot of carefully transferred potted plants were centered on the table on a big tray. (The plants had been moved by hand after having been covered with plastic dry-cleaning bags.)

The two petit-point chairs could sit anywhere in the room—near a couch or one behind the desk. (A beautifully shaped chair is like a piece of sculpture. It can stand anywhere.)

The black Chinese lamp went on top of a long chest that had just managed to fit on a short wall.

The entry hall, emptied of cartons, held the big old hall table waiting for its companion mirror. The two hall chairs huddled up to each side of it. The umbrella stand was nearby.

All extra tables were squeezed against chairs and couches. Extension cords pressed lamps that were not near wall sockets into use. And Cecily wanted to hang the pictures.

"Not yet," I said. "The walls aren't dry enough."

If we had hung the pictures, she would have thought the room was done. And that room—that apartment—was not done. It was managing to survive. Like its occupant.

The handyman departed. Cecily looked around, looked at me, and said, "Looks, uh, cozy . . . doesn't it?"

Crowded would have been the word. But I didn't say it.

I left her as she was putting her good dishes in her breakfront. In exactly the same positions they'd been in before.

Cecily called me the next day to say that she didn't like the furniture arrangement. She'd decided to get rid of the long chest of drawers in the bedroom and use Mat's tall, slender chest of drawers for her things instead. (That was *all* she didn't like?)

The next day she called to say she was leaving.

She was going two thousand miles away to visit her daughter.

But she was going to leave her key for me so that I could come in with fabric samples, because nothing seemed to match. And would her old draperies fit?

Of course I wasn't going to get fabrics to cover all that stuff. And old draperies almost *never* fit. But I wished her a good rest, and told her I'd take care of whatever I could. Which meant I'd do nothing until she took a fresh look at the new place upon her return.

There's nothing like going away to give you some objectivity. It's an expensive way to get a new point of view. In this case, expensive both in money and in emotions. Because when she called to tell me she was back, she was in a state approaching panic.

"Duvie! It's awful! It's so crowded in here. What can we do? I can't look at it. . . ."

"Cecily, remember when you moved? We agreed we'd get

rid of a few things afterward? Remember? All right, calm down. Now is after."

I hoped that by the time I saw her in a couple of days, she would have reached the point of parting with some of her furniture. Her visual "pain" could make her well enough to choose the pieces that could go.

Have you ever seen anybody who is pale under a sun tan? That was Cecily when I got to her apartment.

"Duvie, come in. I've made up my mind about a few things and I'll need your help."

Not only *my* help, I thought privately, but the help of movers again, or of charities who give tax deductions for furniture, or of needy or greedy relatives, or of antique dealers. Probably *all* of them.

By the end of the day, Cecily and I had come to a few conclusions. It took the whole day, because Cecily kept hesitating. It was stop, then go.

Here was our "go" list and the answers to the "stops" that were thrown in along the way:

The dining-room table and chairs would go. Even without its extra leaves, it was a table made for a dining *room*. With its two pedestal bases and oval top, it could seat eight. With its leaves in it, it could serve a sizable part of the Swiss Legation. If, in her new apartment, she invited lots of guests, it would be for a buffet dinner; mostly, she'd have small dinner parties. The eight chairs were not only too many, but too big. Since her children had fully furnished dining rooms, they wouldn't need the dining-room furniture (and she didn't need the mammoth shipping costs). Her favorite charity would give her a large tax deduction for it, with an *appraisal in writing.* They would pick it up, haul it out, and she could use the deduction; most widows need tax deductions, during the first year particularly.

The Utterly Lost Widow

The old den couch would go. It was too large, it needed a new slipcover, and she didn't need *it.* Her living-room couch was a very beautiful piece and comfortable. A couch is a pain in the neck to get rid of. It would go the charity way, and would not bring much in the way of deduction; nothing is more second hand than an old upholstered sofa.

The wing chair would go. This was very hard for her to discard. She knew it was much too large for the room and that it wasn't even particularly comfortable. But it was Mat's chair. She called her son and offered to ship it to him. He said, "Mom, I don't need that chair. . . . Neither do you. It was Dad we loved, not his chair." That wing chair fitted into the antique category, so I decided to see what else might go into the same grouping and call in an antique dealer. (Always try to sell a group of pieces at once; if you lose a little on one thing, you make it up on something else that may be more popular at the moment. Antiques have a tendency to get older—and more valuable. Nice thought.)

The hall table and one of the hall chairs would go. Fairly formal living always breeds fairly formal entry halls. The eye grows accustomed to the standard hall formula. She didn't need it now. What she *did* need was her beautiful former dining-room breakfront. It would be in the entry hall, covering almost the whole wall one saw upon entering. With good lighting, it would greet the guest with a display of lovely china, silver, and choice art objects. To sit on or put something on quickly (which is a hall necessity), we'd use the one hall chair we'd keep. For current mail, we'd get a marble shelf mounted onto a wall right near the door—convenient, but taking up no floor space. Umbrella stand? In the hall guest closet. It really needed to be available only when there was a rainstorm. The hall mirror that lives in almost every entranceway would find itself hung on the narrow wall above the chair, where it would reflect some of that

93

dazzling breakfront. I told Cecily that I thought the old hall pieces should be offered to the antique dealer. I wasn't sure they were antiques, but they were handsome, and if he bought them just because they were attractive, a good buy, and part of a "small load," *he* could always resell them to a not-so-antique-dealer.

Mat's rocker would go, because it was broken. I offered to have it fixed—just one arm was loose. I was hoping she would say no. She haltingly said, "No." I thought it was because of the words of her son. Whatever the reason, I was glad it was leaving, because I didn't want *her* sitting in it again. She didn't need to remember illness. The charity folk would take it.

The large bedroom dresser would be disposed of as per her first request. She had already transferred her drawer-type clothing to Mat's tall slender chest of drawers. As we stood in the bedroom, she said to me, "You're going to say I'm crazy, but I've had a lot of time to think and I don't think I want the twin beds anymore." She was expecting me to object because the bedroom had more space now. But—I have *always* thought—when a woman moves from one type of living to another, she should get a new bed. "Cecily, you're not crazy, but let's be sure you have something to sleep on before we get rid of both beds." (Give away your bed in haste and you can be sure your new bed will not arrive until hope and sleep are totally lost.) But Cecily was ahead of me. She had already promised her newlywed niece the entire bedroom setup, *excluding* the tall chest. Cecily would sleep on her living-room couch, because the bedroom bundle would be picked up that same evening. The entire bonanza would be hauled away by truck and grateful newly-weds. I said, "I take it back, Cecily, you *are* crazy."

Many lamps would light other people's rooms. She had enough lamps to illuminate the reading rooms of several librar-ies. She hesitated about a particular pair of porcelain personages. (Milkmaid and husband. Or milkman?) The kids, she said, had always loved them. Great! Send one to the son and one to the daughter. I, as Solomon, came up with that judgment. She, as Noah, thought in pairs, so they would be shipped undivided to her daughter. Another fine brass student lamp would go to her son. The newlyweds were underlit (they always are), so she'd give them a couple of lamps "as long as they're hiring that expensive truck." There were plenty left. Including the black Chinese lamp and shade, of course.

A firescreen, andirons, and a pair of elaborate wall sconces would enchant the antique dealer. Cecily didn't have a fireplace, nor the need for the fancy candleholders. (Interesting item: she and Mat had purchased them on a European tour. She said, "I always secretly hated them. But Mat loved them . . . so, I . . . anyway, the kids never liked them, either." She laughed softly, and continued, "Wonder how many things Mat lived with just because *I* loved them?")

After the departure of furnishings, objects, old draperies, a dessert service for twelve, and six cartons of pots, pans, and waffle irons, Cecily called me to say she was "ready to go" again.

As I was about to say, "Please don't go away and come back to disaster *again,*" she explained that she was ready to go shopping for fabrics and "arrange the rooms and get carpeting, and . . . and . . ."

"First arrange the rooms," I told that energetic lady. When your room arrangements are set up comfortably, then you can start worrying about colors and yardages.

The rooms were easy to arrange. Because now there actually wasn't enough practical furniture. We were missing a dining setup and a bed, for starters. She'd been eating on her card table, using one of her set of folding bridge chairs. And she swore she was sleeping in great comfort on her living-room sofa.

"Besides," she said, walking extremely erectly, "I love all this feeling of space."

Space was the key. When you move from a large home to a small one—even after dumping the unnecessary furnishings—the sense of space is what you miss most. You suffer from lost rooms.

So, seeing as how she'd grown accustomed to sleeping on a couch, and that she was down to one slender chest of drawers and two chairs in bedroom furniture, I suggested we buy a handsome convertible sofa and turn the bedroom into a library.

Such glee! Bookcases went against the former bed wall. The desk from the living room went in front of the big bedroom window. The two upholstered French armchairs were angled in a corner, separated by an exquisite round table topped with marble. And *that* glorious grouping would face her soon-to-be-ordered sleep sofa.

Another former living-room table would serve as her bed-time necessity table next to the couch. It had a lower shelf—good for radio, Kleenex, etc. Its inlaid wood top would hold an elegant lamp and her phone.

Her tall chest of drawers fitted onto a narrow wall near her impeccable closet. On its top we placed her fine collection of delft apothecary jars. (Large art objects on top of a tall chest give a handsome "unbedroomy" look.)

The paintings she loved most would be in her personal room. Hung at odd levels along the whole couch wall, for good viewing.

Lamps of great beauty lit the room evenly. Their three-way bulbs enabled her to control the light intensity. The lamp that served as her night-table lighting would have a switch installed on its cord, so she wouldn't have to fumble under a lampshade in the dark.

The two upholstered French armchairs were our clues to

color. Recently redone, they were fresh and vibrant: striped satin in blue and green on white. Now that we had the whole bedroom done mentally, we would order the sleep couch in a color taken from our clues—and we could decide on carpeting and draperies. Simple, speedy, efficient? No, Ma'am, when all your rooms need "doing," ordering carpeting and draperies for one room at a time is insane.

But the convertible sofa had to be chosen and ordered immediately. Because, unless you find a couch for immediate sale in exactly the color and style you want, you are going to have to wait for delivery. And wait and wait. The showroom for sleep couches put up with my drilling Cecily on how to open and shut the bed: "Squat, don't pull, lift the mechanism gently—it's made to *glide* open." Then I made her lie down on the slender mattress. "Is it really firm? When it's shut, can you lift off the two seat cushions easily?" Yes, because two cushions are easier to handle than one. She glanced around the showroom after her practice sessions and saw a French day bed. Two high side arms, and loose back cushions on a mattress. Her eyes lit up! "Nothing doing, Cecily—you'll have to make it up from start to finish every night. The closed convertible can keep its sheets and blanket *on.*"

We ordered the convertible in double-bed size—just a shade under six feet—to be upholstered in a pale blue velvet. It had a squarish pattern cut into the fabric, so it picked up light and shadow, but wouldn't show soil. A contemporary but classic couch. Also expensive. We were told to expect it in six weeks. "Aim for twelve," I told Cecily, "then think how tickled you'll be when it comes in only nine weeks."

Cecily, one of the wall-to-wall-carpet-lovers, wasn't changing her mind. She liked the feel of carpet underfoot, the muffled sound, the solid flow of color. Carpeting needs to be measured expertly. So we had to make our living-room and hall color decisions, too, then choose the carpeting and do some more waiting. After the measuring men came, we'd have to wait for the carpet to arrive and for the installers to install it.

The living room and hall contained furniture that was not only elegant but old. Her couch was a silk damask, the color of cranberries. She wanted it redone. But it didn't need it. Yes, it was old, but it had aged evenly. There were no worn sections or frays, no spots. "Hold it," I said, "let's see what else needs doing, because the carpet color may tone the whole place up."

Her two petit-point chairs were alive with warm colors and their freshly polished frames were perfect.

The only upholstered pieces remaining were the love seat and a small easy chair. The love seat had been in the old bedroom and looked it. Tiny flowers and leaves and weensie stripes in ivories, pinks, and greens. The easy chair was a dark gray velvet. They were the worn-out color culprits.

"Cecily, what goes great with cranberries?"

"Turkey," and she looked at me as if I'd gone mad.

"What color is good turkey on a plate?"

"Duvie—it's light, uh, off-white, almost beige. Are you hungry, dear?"

She didn't know whether to feed me or commit me. But we'd found the color for the love seat and easy chair. Off-white— we'd do them in a nubby raw silk. They'd be a delicious team. We'd have them deeply tufted and skirted so they'd match and wouldn't look boxy. And so we called the upholsterer and he was disappointed because there was so little to do. What could have been a mammoth job had become a small one.

The carpet colors? In this case, one carpet color throughout. For maximum-space look. A soft gold. It would warm up the cool blues and whites of the bedroom-library and let the antique tones of the living-dining room melt together. (Gold carpeting is for good housekeepers: it shows dirt quickly. But we had chosen a deep-pile acrylic that was supposedly easy to keep clean. It was so plush-velvety-looking that it wouldn't show dirt badly anyway. But everything gets dirty eventually. So everything needs to be maintained.)

We found we didn't need a dining table. The long, slender refectory table would serve splendidly. We ordered cane-backed chairs in an almost-matching wood. Their seats would be upholstered in off-white leather, so they could be at home anywhere in the apartment.

The bedroom, newly christened the "library," needed draperies to keep out the light. We chose a white permanent-glaze chintz that was patterned with blue, green, and gold drifting summer flowers. Like all good non-sheer draperies, they were lined.

The living-dining room, which was fast becoming the "drawing room," didn't need to be shielded from light.

We used a gold similar to the carpet color and ordered very full draperies of casement fabric. (That means anything sheer, from pure thin silk to fiberglass. I like dacron ninon. It's washable, hangs well, and feels silky to the touch.)

You may have gathered that all these projected ideas took a little time to achieve—if "a little time" means six months.

In between, Cecily had shopped for her bathroom, her children, and the latest cookbooks. She had also shopped for an orthopedist and a back brace.

All the time she had spent sleeping on her "comfortable living-room couch" had not aided a back condition she rarely mentioned. The convertible sofa, which *had* arrived on time, did not improve the situation. She told *me* not to worry: "When my back is really bad, I just leave the convertible open and have the handyman slip a bedboard under the mattress."

It was *my* fault. I should have let her have the French day bed. It might have been a chore to make up nightly, but it could have had a firm, solid mattress and no mechanism to have to fuss with. So I'll state it flatly: if you're a minute over thirty or have ever had one back twinge, don't use a convertible couch for steady sleeping.

That gracious Cecily, who should have hit me over the head, greeted me at her door and said, "Thank you for giving me this lovely apartment."

And it was lovely. One room flowed to another. The entry hall glowed golden from the crystal chandelier lighting the carpet. The great breakfront glittered. The hall chair was in cranberry velvet.

The living room was one sweeping expanse, now that its furnishings were against the walls with ease; over the couch hung the ancestral portraits in their great gold frames. Her coffee table was splendid with its porcelain bowl filled with apples. The love seat and easy chair across the room "belonged."

The dining table was lit by an old chandelier that had colored crystal fruits suspended from its bronze framework.

Each classically arranged piece was polished perfection.

Walking into the bedroom-library, you thought you were in a large house with many rooms beyond. The idea had worked. If you've got a library, surely you must have other rooms!

All the lamps, from the magnificent pair of matched bronzes on each side of the cranberry couch to the carved jade on a small chest, had new shades. Simple silks—some flared—one pleated.

Only one lamp—standing on a table near the golden-draperied window wall and lighting a mass of plants—had an old shade on it. The black Chinese lamp. You see, *it* didn't need a new shade.

All it needed was a new place to live.

Like Cecily.

5

The Husband-Angler

"It's not even worth talking about . . ." and so she continued talking about it.

"I mean, really, there's not a *thing* left to be said, it's *so* ridiculous. . . ."

Since there was nothing left to be said and the worthless subject was ridiculous, I knew I was in for a long evening.

The worthless subject: MEN

The ridiculous idea: MARRIAGE

There she was, sitting on my couch, eating pretzels out of my bowl, and establishing herself as my new client. She had seen a small apartment I had decorated for a friend of hers. She liked it. She wanted one like it. But different.

And it certainly was going to be different. Because after two and a half hours, we still hadn't discussed her new apartment. It's a good idea to choose a decorator because you like a place the decorator has done. In fact, I think it's the only way to choose one. But it's also nuts not to tell the new decorator the way you want to live.

Surely she didn't expect her apartment to be a duplicate of her friend's. For one thing, the friend was a much older woman. For another, her friend was very rich. So I figured—maybe she wanted her new place to look like "old money"?

You see, if I can't get definite requests out of a client, I have to do some detective work on my own. I watch. And listen.

I watched and listened. She was attractive. She was wearing an almost totally blue outfit. (Expensive.) She had a good job with an advertising agency. She worked mostly with men. (Mostly married men.) And that's as far as I could get, because the one-sided conversation stayed on men, and marriage. And how most men were married already. And how dumb it was even to think about marriage.

Finally, I managed to say, "There are a group of men who are not married. I believe they are called 'single men.' Sometimes, 'bachelors.' . . . And how would you like a mostly blue apartment?"

"Oh, I can't *stand* blue. But I mean—you know—marrying a man would mean giving up everything. Freedom. The opportunity to expand. And develop myself. To move around as I wish . . ."

"Speaking of moving, shouldn't we start making some plans for your new apartment?" There, I'd said it. After only three hours, I had deftly managed to get the conversation back to decorating.

"But," and she hesitated, "what would happen if I got my new apartment all done and then decided to get married?"

"It's happened before. He moves in. Or you move out. You both live together somewhere, as husband and wife. It's been going on for years."

She looked up at me. Her eyes were as blue as her shirt. (The color she couldn't stand?) And very clearly she said, "Not for me it hasn't. I haven't had anything anywhere near like marriage going on for years . . . or even months."

So marriage was what she wanted. And what she needed was an apartment to attract a husband. Not somebody else's husband, but a single bachelor unmarried man willing to change status. There *are* such things. Both the special type of apartment and the special type of man.

Now, I may be a truly great detective but I'm not hoping to win any awards for outstanding bravery. For instance, I knew what she wanted—and, deep down, she knew what she wanted —but I couldn't come right out and tell her. She would have been embarrassed. And probably would have hated me—as well as herself for being so transparent.

So all I had to do was get her on the track leading to the special apartment she needed and get her off the idea behind its creation. To build an apartment to possibly attract a future husband, the husband hunter must be relaxed, and must please herself, first; mostly, she must *not* be a nervous wreck. Any nervous-wreck single woman is headed straight for a nervous-wreck apartment, and has every possibility of attracting a nervous-wreck male companion.

There were several things I needed to know in order for us to get started. Did she have an apartment already picked out? Was she moving with a great many possessions? Would she need me as her decorator full-time? Could I serve her as well by just hourly consultations at the new place? Could she get some time off from her job for trips to showrooms or shops?

If I work as a part-time decorator on an hourly-fee basis, I leave the client with sketches, directions on places to go, color samples of stuff—and she's free to shop on her own, and sometimes to know the joys of hiring her own workmen. Also, I'm not around to watch installations, paint jobs, cabinetmaking—all the noncreative and soul-searing aspects of doing interiors.

I don't know about other decorators, but *I* would rather work on an hourly basis—and duck out when the frenzy begins.

Just as I was about to tell her how much money she'd save by using me as visiting seer, she said to me, "Mrs. Clark, I've been saving money for a long time and I really do want the full decorator treatment. My job is a new promotion and it takes a lot of time because I want to prove myself. . . . I'm in an office full of men, you know."

I'd gathered as much.

Okay, so I got a lined-paper pad for her new folder. Her name would go on the top of the folder. And inside: notes on the job, specifications, copies of order forms. This goes into a shopping bag eventually, which will hold fabric and rug samples, small rolls of wallpaper pieces, and little paint-color chips. (And, sometimes, an apple for me.)

With pad in hand and glasses sliding off my nose, I think I look very efficient and businesslike. When I look like this, the new client answers questions speedily. (Somehow they think they've gotten into an unusual cab and the meter's running.)

Questions and answers from first interview with the (unbeknownst to herself) husband hunter:

Q. "Present address?"

A. "403 East Fifty-third Street. Apt. 2A."

Q. "New address?"

A. "Same."

Q. "Huh?"

A. "Oh, I knew I forgot to tell you something. I'm already in my new apartment."

Q. "How many rooms and how much furniture do you have?"

A. Two and a half and a bed."

End of formal question-and-answer ceremony.

"Listen, I hate to sound idiotic and unprofessional, but what is a two-and-a-half-room apartment these days? I haven't decorated one in years and the room counts seem to have changed. Landlords today either count oddly or I can't tell a whole room from a half of one."

Her two and a half? "One living room with an alcove in it, a *table notes !*

small dressing room leading to a bath, squarish entry with a 'dash' of a kitchen directly opposite the front door." Sounded more like one and seven-eighths.

Damn the mathematics and full speed ahead.

"And the bed you've got, is it an heirloom or something?"

"I guess you might call it an heirloom—it's been in the family a long time. It's a folding cot."

So we were starting on a full furnishing and accessorizing job, with maybe a few other things like paint and paper and curtaining and rugs and on and on. . . .

She had said she wanted the full decorator treatment. That didn't necessarily mean she intended to spend a lot of money. A lot of money to one person can mean very little money to another. I always ask how much a new client wants to spend. I never get a real answer. Besides, I can't tell anyone, honestly, how much a total job will cost. I have to find out what kinds of things they like. French or English antiques make me think money. Danish modern and foam-rubber slab sofas with a few choice plastic pieces thrown in—well, they let me know it's tight money.

So when I see the first signs of money panic occur after I show a choice fabric sample, I always say, "Yell when you think you're running out of money and we'll wait awhile on some things."

If you're hoping your apartment will be temporary, you shouldn't spend *big* money on: built-ins, carpeting, fancy draperies.

These items, though perhaps necessary, can be faked. The important thing is that they look good. Do as my new client did, who was independent, successful, and on her own: a single young woman testing the inside truth. She faked courage.

And that's perfectly normal. Moving is difficult enough when your plans are definite. Moving is terrible when you're trying to design your life as well as your décor.

The Not So Terrible Move

So I told her as the elevator door shut, "Decorating can be fun." It is such a dreadful cliché we both laughed.

We met at the front door of her new apartment a few days later. It was early evening. She'd just gotten home from work. She begged my pardon, because she was "grabbing a bite." If you *can* "bite" into yogurt. Of course I was offered some, but I said I'd prefer a cup of coffee. "Got it for you!" she said cheerfully as she whipped into the kitchenette, dipped into a grocery bag on a counter top, and pulled out a paper container.

When I take my dose of hemlock, I shall use a paper container. So I asked for a regular cup to pour the coffee into. "Haven't got one," said she. "A mug will do just fine," I responded cautiously. She didn't have one of those, either. Made mental note: have feeling this lady can't cook.

Now we had to go over the apartment, inch by inch. I took out my steel tape measure, which stretches for twelve feet, weighs a little under a ton, and reels itself back into position with a snap designed to take off a leg. Always use a steel tape measure with great care and with the help of another person to hold the end of it in place. As you fight over who's reading it correctly, when it's all expanded, check to see if you added on the usual two inches that the tape container itself measures. Never use a cloth tape measure. They curl, stretch, or go crooked. A yardstick is rotten, too, because though they give you 36 inches of solid wood, they will do you no good in a sealed-in area of, say, 33½ inches. I also loathe those flexible, folding wood measures. (I never unfold them in order, so the numbers aren't in proper sequence, which leads to "fits" and misfits.)

We started by measuring her "squarish" entry. It turned out to be a rectangular space of six feet by nine feet. "Really?" she said incredulously. "It seemed so much smaller to me."

Rooms often seem smaller without furniture in them. The

The Husband-Angler

reason is your eyes. They focus on the walls. With no distraction, the walls appear to be closer to you. In this particular instance, after you walked in the front door you looked straight ahead into the lighted kitchenette, so you lost the intervening floor space. She took all this in with the same gusto she obviously derived from her prune-whip yogurt.

The living room with its alcove was large. And I mean it. Her apartment was in a town house, and two rooms had obviously been used to create the new large room and its alcove—with the dressing room and bath beyond. Other lovely benefits were the high ceilings, nice woodwork, and the two long separated windows that faced the street just at treetop level. The spring twilight filtered into the room through a mass of quivering leaves.

"That's lovely, isn't it . . . just seeing the leaves," she said. "I'd like to keep it that way. . . . you know, no curtains."

"If you can arrange to keep spring and summer, it's a fine idea. But when winter comes you'll have bare branches and sudden neighbors if you don't have curtains. No view in this world doesn't need curtaining off occasionally. Black nights, bleak weather, even the glory of a noonday sun can become a bore or a threat. You always have to use something to shield your windows."

"Then you know what?" she said, "I'd like to have organdy curtains with big ruffles—really feminine—tied back and very full, and . . ." She stopped. Possibly because she had seen the expression on my face. (I try not to have facial expressions, but I've never once succeeded.)

"Don't be upset," I said, "because you've given me the first hint of what we both need to know. You want a feminine apartment. So now we can really start with the decorating plans. Okay? Answer me fast. When was the last time *you* felt the most feminine? . . . Fast!"

The Not So Terrible Move

"At . . . at a key club! . . . That's the damn truth!"

"What did it look like?"

She paused momentarily, then said, laughing, "A men's club . . . with bunnies."

"In other words, the femininity was supplied by the female occupants, right? They showed up against the darkish, masculine background."

"Wow! You going to make this place into a dark bar-and-grill, with me in black mesh stockings?"

We laughed ourselves onto the same wave-length: her apartment would be designed to show her off. Actually, there should be no such thing as a completely feminine or masculine home. If it looks as if it's pushing toward one or the other, the strain will show mostly on its inhabitant. A woman is a woman. A man is a man. Decorating is only the comfortably beautiful background for sexiness.

Since I've decorated for women with men on their minds before, I had a special few things in my shopping bag. I never bring a lot of samples the first time, or any time. One of the blessings of having a decorator is that you have fewer decisions to make, because the decorator has been over the territory before you. Even if you're working on your own, limit the amounts of samples you bring home. Too many are too much. You can always go get more.

I showed her a paint-sample chip of warm, creamy brown. Not extremely dark, but far from beige. It's called "mocha" this year.

"How about this—with white ceilings and white woodwork?"

She had a hard time seeing it; daylight had evaporated and we were using the only floor lamp she had—one of those pole lamps with three spotlight fixtures on it.

Before she went blind from staring at the small chip (don't stare at a small colored paint chip too long), I pulled out a fabric sample she might like, so she could relax into the mocha color by seeing how it went with something else.

"Say, that's a nice shade of brown—it's soft but not too soft—and that piece of material really does show up against it. All that white keeps the brown fresh-looking."

I handed her three large fabric samples. I never show those little postage-stamp-size pieces of fabric called "swatches." Each large fabric sample I showed her featured mostly white, because the other paint-sample chips I had secreted in the depths of my shopping bag were all dark shades. (Since she liked the brown, she would never even see the others.)

The fabrics (all drapery or slipcover weight):

1. A classic toile of black on white. A toile is a pattern featuring shepherds and shepherdesses gamboling around under trees and behind bushes. This particular one had lots of contrast in its black-and-white scattered drawings. (Very popular during the time of Louis XVI, toiles will remain popular when we're on another planet, living under a glass dome. Because they're elegant and go with anything.)

2. A daring dramatic modern floral very clearly drawn in bright colors—blues, yellows, oranges, pinks, browns—lots of black—all against white. It was beautifully designed. Remember, the print on a piece of fabric should be just as well drawn as on a picture you might choose. (A lilac may be a good shade of lilac, but if the lilac itself isn't well drawn it'll always be a bad lilac.)

3. A big blatant bold plaid. Done with brush strokes. Hot pinks, bright yellows, black, and browns weaving across each other over a white background and with enough drama to demand audience attention. (She would hate it or applaud it.)

The three fabric choices were vastly different from one another, but any one of them could go with a dark-walled room.

Her choice would be my guide to the style of room she could live in happily. (Not one of them was overwhelmingly feminine, you may have noticed.)

She fooled around with the samples. I told her the prices and she didn't flinch at the really expensive one. She even kept coming back to one of them. So I removed it from the others and placed it against the paint chip. It was very dramatic there. And the least expensive—and the best of the lot, because it would give us free reign on everything else.

She chose the black-and-white toile.

Against the mocha brown, the black and white was stunning. What could have been merely "safe" became startling. Brown walls with black and white to start us off.

"Man!" she said.

Exactly what I was thinking.

"How about wall-to-wall carpeting in a deeper shade of this brown tone? Against the white woodwork at the walls' bottoms, it'll be as if the carpet was surrounded by a bright white border." I asked this as I produced a sample of carpet. It was the size of a large Band-Aid. She'd have to go to the carpet showroom to see a larger sample; I can't carry them (and often can't get them).

The carpeting was cheap. But, remember, when you buy inexpensive carpeting—aside from the fact that it won't wear for very long—the price that attracts you may not include lining and installation.

So though you love the color, be sure you ask the price. Installed! She loved the color. But she wanted to know what the carpet was made of. "A man-made fiber." (Whatever happened to wool? I don't really know. But there is less and less of it being shown. I shall not even go into the sales talk that comes with the new "miracle fibers." Until the Bible adds amendments, *I* shall just believe in the old miracles.) By the time we'd have the carpeting lined with foam-rubber padding, no one would know how thin it was.

"Only one thing," she said as she gazed at her capsule-carpet sample, "I've always wanted a real thick, fluffy rug—shaggy—you know?"

"They mat badly, get really tramped down, and their prices have done just the reverse." Which is almost, but not quite true. I don't think any man should feel as if he's sinking into carpeting; it's a very trapped feeling. What he doesn't know, he shouldn't have to guess from having his ankles encased.

Now that our backgrounds were behind us in planning, I aimed at the most important item: the bed. Since she was already ensconced in her alcove with its folding cot, that's where she wanted to sleep. The alcove faced the windows.

"You *sure* you want to sleep there?"

"Yup, makes me feel all cuddly and safe."

Very nice way to feel.

Everyone should have the most comfortable bed possible. She needed a bed that was not only comfortable, but sittable, inviting, easy to maintain, and beautiful. She wanted a convertible couch. So because of past experiences with the same, I had to ask her a group of questions that sounded as if I were compiling a medical chart.

"Are you under thirty?"

"Yes," she said, astonished.

"You got a good back?"

"Yes! . . . To say nothing of a passable front and great legs! Have you lost your mind?"

"No, I just want to be sure you can survive the rigors of a convertible couch. Because if you hadn't answered 'yes' to those questions, we would have had to dream up a glorious day bed or couch-bed." And I explained about the thin mattresses and opening and shutting mechanisms inherent in convertible couches.

Despite the fact that she told me she swam weekly at a health club and did exercises daily, I told her we were going to spend money on the couch. We were not going to get the sleekest one or the one that looked least like a convertible. We'd aim for the convertible that concealed the thickest, firmest mattress, which meant it might look bulky from the side. (That wouldn't show, anyway, because it would be in the alcove.)

We'd order the couch in a white tweedy fabric. After she said "It'll show the dirt," I told her it would be sprayed against staining, it would have big extra cushions (not those little cookie throw cushions), which would really be her own soft bed pillows with zip-off cases. (Fewer storage problems.)

That white couch with its soft accessories would say for my client, "I'm not worried about dirt—make yourself comfortable." Worrying about dirt is the single outstanding hobby of most women; if it gets out of hand, it can keep a woman single.

The minute we were done discussing the couch, she said, "Coffee table." "Save your money," I said, "you don't need one. All you need is a tray on a folding stand. You can use the tray all the time, and when you really need a coffee table at a party, put the tray on the tray stand." (And no one would have to assume the "gold-panning position" used to reach most low coffee-table levels.)

A coffee table is a couch-blocker. And for reasons I was not willing to admit to her at the moment, I didn't want anything blocking the use of that couch.

Speaking of coffee and trays and guests led us to another necessity. A dining table and chairs.

Her eyes drifted toward the entry hall with its kitchen door. "In there?"

The Husband-Angler

After having proved to her that her entry was bigger than she thought, I had to admit it was too small.

"It's too small. You don't want people all cramped up. Look at the space you've got in this living room. Think of how pretty a table and chairs would look in front of one window—you'll see it when you enter the room."

"But I—uh—wasn't thinking of having *lots* of people."

If you don't have lots of people in for parties, you are not likely to reduce the number to one. The important one.

"If you have a small table in the hall for mail, magazines, and such, you can eat off it, too. That kitchen won't hold you and your yogurt *and* a chair, you know."

All of a sudden, it occurred to her that four dining chairs would be four more chairs than she now owned. She walked over to the window that framed her beloved tree and said, "It *would* be nice to sit here."

So via the desire for seating space and a view, I convinced her that she needed a 42-inch round dining table. And a hall table.

A traditional table in a traditional room? No. She was a modernist, really. Her clothes, her job, her wit—all showed it. She wanted glass and chrome. And the choice couldn't have been better. The glass tabletop in front of the window would reflect the sky. Easy to clean, too.

You can get a round glass dining table with a chrome base for very little money. But watch out for the real bargains. The very cheap ones have very thin glass tops; you'll feel as if you're leaning on a flexible razor blade. Ask for a thicker glass top, and be ready to spend money on the thicker glass.

The dining chairs must be very comfortable, because they would be used all over the place. "Go sit around," I told her. "Chose any kind of chair you want. Any period will do well in this room and with that table. But we must be sure it's a long-

113

distance runner, that it can be sat in, lolled in, and pushed around."

I gave her one other instruction on the right chair: don't choose anything with a slick plastic seat. (Men's pants stick to the bottom and they're always secretly inspecting for a rear-crotch tear when they hear that sudden ripping sound upon rising from the chair. We'd order the seat cover in a fabric.)

We marched into the hall where her other table would be, on the wall next to the kitchen door. We had over four feet of wall space, so we could have a longish, slim table and maybe a dining-height bench underneath it. We'd look for a table in the glass-and-chrome division again.

"And think of it," I said, "you can actually set up a buffet in here and then have your company eat off your dining table as well as their laps!"

The moment of truth was fast upon us. We were standing next to the kitchen door and discussing food.

"Duvie, you know I can't cook. At least, I *think* you know."

"Yes."

"So, what's all this business about dining and serving?"

"If you can read the back of a can of cream-of-mushroom soup, you can cook." I'm firmly convinced that half the young women of America were launched into gourmet cooking through the medium of a mushroom-soup can recipe for tuna-fish casserole. (Sometimes you have to read through several cans for that particular one, but along the way you'll get other recipes utilizing this amazing mushroom soup. I think you can eat a towel if you soak it in hot cream-of-mushroom soup.)

Then, after you've tried the back-of-the-can method and have proved to yourself that you're a good reader, go to a bookshop and ask for the cookbook section. This will cover a mile and a half of shelf space. All you have to do is tell the salesperson that you want a basic cookbook for beginners. If you're embarrassed, you can ask to have it gift-wrapped.

I don't care if you know how to defrost a TV dinner in ten seconds. That's not cooking. You've got to know how to have an undippy hors-d'oeuvres tray, how to make a decent salad, and how to prepare a couple of casserole dishes. You can't fool yourself into comfortable entertaining. Cooking will help you feel at home with guests. (And, as you may have noticed, men *eat.*)

We were standing in the kitchen during my song of praise to a soup can and a simple cookbook. It was a galley-type kitchen: equipment lined against two walls, with a narrow walkway between. Plenty of storage space. All new. The high ceiling featured a fluorescent-light fixture. A blank wall faced us at the far end; you could see it from the entrance.

"I feel like I'm in a surgery . . . as the patient," she said, looking at the all-white, all-intimidating space.

"You ever been in a surgery that had cabinets sprayed pale pink, with flowers, butterflies, and leaves on the ceiling and walls?"

"That sounds like a bedroom!"

The kitchen in the apartment of the lady who longs to be a wife should be the most feminine spot in the house. If it's reminiscent of Du Barry's boudoir, then the lady obviously spends a lot of time in there; therefore she must be a great cook. (She may be in there reading soup cans. But not for long, because she's going to *like* being in there, and she can't spend all her time smelling the flowers on the wallpaper, either. So she'll cook.)

While she was visualizing her sexy kitchen, I was telling her to go to a discount department store that stocked cookware, dinnerware, glassware, and silverware.

The Not So Terrible Move

"When you find the store, look for the most mature saleslady. Tell her you're just setting up housekeeping and you need simple cooking and serving items."

If the money outlay seems like a lot to you, compare the cost to a good spring suit. Your pots, pans, and plates will outlast any suit.

We left the kitchen and decided that if it was going to be so beautiful we should give the kitchen door back to the landlord. An interior kitchen may have the best ventilator in the world, but the odds are the door will be left open all the time for extra ventilation. Or to prevent small attacks of claustrophobia. All kitchens get littered counter-tops and potted stoves. So we decided on a set of louvered doors. Her kitchen door would be a pair of white shutters.

We'd hang them well above floor level to just above normal eye level. Short doors, because, remember, kitchens are messy mostly at waistline height. We'd be covering the clutter while showing the pretty pinks and leafy paper, and the white wrought-iron lighting fixture that would replace the glaring fluorescent tubes. (Measure the light fixture you choose so that you're sure it won't get hit by upper kitchen-cabinet doors.)

Since the whole kitchen effect was the first thing the entering guest would see, we had to have a fine-looking kitchen floor. We couldn't use the brown foyer carpeting, so I suggested dark wood parquet made of vinyl. A costly one, but a small kitchen floor can be made of expensive materials because you don't need much of it.

There were two closets in her entrance hall, to the left of the front door. One was big. The other was guest size. (Big enough for one fat guest or six thin coats.) I suggested we turn the guest closet into a bar. She wouldn't miss a closet she'd never used. Surely, between the closet space in her dressing room and the large hall closet, a single woman would have enough room for clothes. (And, it occurred to me, there wasn't enough closet space for a transient male. The amount of closet she was willing to share would be up to her.)

After she pondered the bar idea, she decided she really liked it, because it would make the entrance hall bigger. No door—just the white doorframe would remain—and we'd extend the hall carpeting right into the closet. The closet light would be covered with a small lantern. We'd remove the usual hat shelf and paint the walls to match the hall. It would be an open wine cellar. Stackable narrow wine racks would go up one side, leaving plenty of space for a deep, serving-height glass shelf. This would be of heavy glass, hung on fat brackets. Another glass shelf would be hung well above it—only deep enough for one row of glasses, so that she wouldn't conk her head when she was mixing a drink. (Or when *he* was mixing a drink, because she didn't know exactly how to do that, either. Of course she could buy a bartender's book, but men guests love to mix specials.)

The removal of a hall closet made us go back through the living room and into her dressing room. It was spacious enough for the vast double closet on one side, and had room on the opposite wall for a chest of some kind. (The bathroom door faced you as you entered from the living room.)

I asked if it was all right if I opened her closet. It was. In it were clothes, neatly hung. And lots of cartons on the floor. Big suitcases were on the upper shelf.

"What's in all the cartons?" I asked.

"Oh, some things I've had."

Before I knew it, she was pulling out the cartons and opening them.

There were carefully wrapped souvenirs from trips: little ashtrays attesting to the fact that there are famous hotels everywhere, little vases featuring windmills and designed to hold one sprig of parsley, teacups and saucers covered with roses, pansies, violets—all guaranteed to choke a teabag—and a selection of minuscule pink porcelain boxes—snuff-type, one nostril only.

Many single women seem to bring home only the souvenirs that can be packed in a Dixie cup. (Men don't like teensie things they're afraid to touch.)

But now I knew she liked porcelain objects.

Another carton had family photographs. Some already framed, some loose. From her face, I could see that she cherished them.

"Let's reframe the ones you love most and hang them in your dressing room on all the exposed wall space."

Personal picture portraits should hang, but not in the main traffic areas. Everyone knows you didn't hatch from a mango pit, and they're not one bit interested in your Uncle Charlie's monocle.

The next box revealed a pair of brass candlesticks. Old and lovely. Her grandmother's. She was so pleased with my enthusiasm, and I was so pleased that she owned memorabilia. More items appeared: a glittering large cut-glass fruit bowl, a slim silver cigarette box, and two long rolled-up scrolls. Chinese paintings on rice paper. Old, distinguished, and kind of gloomy. But quality.

And she had three cartons of books. "How to": Do everything to make yourself skeletal. Do your face over without surgery, etc., etc.

Among this trove were seven volumes of sailing books. She was an ardent and accomplished sailor. This would definitely be important in designing our new riggings.

As they say, "Know thyself." True. But some things about yourself you can keep to yourself. Nobody needs to know you're devoted to your body. But an active hobbyist is fascinating.

So I helped her repack her improvement books and we went

back into the living room. We had two long end walls that would need furnishing.

"How about real captains' chests for your clothing and linen storage?" (I am an ardent devotee of captains' chests. They are the campaign chests that went to sea. Their squared-off corners with brass fittings, the gleaming indented handles—whether reproductions or originals, lacquered black or in a wood finish, or in color, there's not a home in the world they won't fit into with ease.) I hoped she could have authentic, old ones. They're expensive but available, and she needed something of true value. Especially since this kind of antique was part of a real interest she had.

We would probably need two long ones for real drama—*and* real storage space. She was happy about the idea. Worried about the cost.

"If you spend money on antiques, you can't lose in the long run. Because they continue getting older and more valuable. For now, we'll cut back on something else. Bookcases, for instance."

Since she hadn't even been thinking about bookcases, she didn't grasp the savings right off.

Any interesting woman reads. What she reads is a tip-off to what she is—or hopes to be. A bookcase is essential. For one thing, it holds books. For another (and I couldn't tell her this little fact), it's a man-impresser.

She agreed that we had one whole wall to fill; it was the one on the left as you entered the living room.

The cheapest way to fill a wall, practically, is with bookcases. We could get unpainted ones—several narrowish ones—fairly high. And have them painted to match the walls. They wouldn't have to be "installed." They could be moved around. They could be replaced. They could go to a new house. Or they could be thrown out. Go for cheap. What counts in this kind of bookcase is what's on the shelves.

On her shelves? Her sailing books. Cookbooks. A decent encyclopedia set. A huge dictionary. Anything controversial that interested her. Favorite books from childhood. Poetry. Religion. Several new novels—no sex manuals (because she didn't need them). Her bookcase would be reference material. It would bring back memories.

In order to read, she'd need lighting. Her couch niche was large enough for the couch, and two end tables to hold lamps. Forget matching end tables. They look too finicky; "finicky" is the real difference between old-maidish and feminine. Feminine is unfinicky; it may be carefully planned, but not rigidly planned. Cosseted. Not corseted.

Since one end table must serve as her night table, it should have a lower shelf and a big enough top for her phone, lamp, clock-radio, and whatever else she needed nocturnally. We'd use a table-height single bookcase from the unfinished-wood furniture store. We'd have a larger round top cut for it. We'd cover the whole thing with a piece of colored felt; felt comes very wide, so cutting a circle is a cinch. We'd split the front of the felt skirt so that she could reach in for the cleansing tissues, the night cream, the bed socks, the nose drops, etc., that might be stashed on the bottom shelf. A thin plate-glass top would be used to cover the felt surface.

The other table could be smaller. Maybe a plain pedestal base with a black marble top. (Yes, marble stains, but if you get a busy-patterned one no one will ever notice it.) The whole idea? Someone running around shoving coasters under glasses is a pain.

I suggested white lamp bases. Against the brown of the walls the contrast would be good. Copies of Chinese porcelains are available in carloads. Which means they're cheap. We'd get two of the same height, but of different and simple design. Their shades, however, would match even if it meant replacing one of them. And they should be translucent lampshades. Translucent means the light shows through. (As in silk, or rayon, or plastic, or glass.) Opaque means the light doesn't show through. (As in heavy paper or metal.)

She'd need one large dramatic lamp for her captains' chests, which would be almost seven feet long. Or she *could* use a matched pair there. I tentatively suggested using Grandma's brass candlesticks for lamp bases.

She untentatively suggested that she'd smash me with one or both of them if I did. Decorators have a tendency to make a lamp out of anything that doesn't fight back. So if you're a purist, stand your ground.

I graciously retreated, while saying, "Okay, you unimaginative clod—I've got a lamp in my closet you'll *adore*. It was my antique dealer's grandmother's vase. It's huge. It's electrocuted. And it's brilliant Bristol blue."

There was a short pause. As in a duel.

Then she said, "Love to see it. Blue should be gorgeous in here. . . . And that's what counts!" (She didn't know it, but she was the winner.)

Then we talked of more lighting. For dining, she needed more than Grandma's candlesticks. (I secretly believe men hate dining by candlelight; they get too warm. Besides, they often have reason not to trust any food they can't see.) A chandelier hung over the dining table in front of the window would light not only the edibles, but the nearby bookcase and the toile draperies.

Thanks to new hardware and light cords that snake in and out of flexed chain, one can hang a chandelier anywhere today (as long as there's a floor plug nearby). Just remember the one who does it should be a trusted handyman. Not necessarily an electrician—but that would be even better.

"How about something in front of the other window?" she asked, having already approved of a tall slender mirror for the wall between the two windows.

"What you really need *in* that window is an air conditioner." (Men hate heat.)

It was early spring, soon it would be summer, and the price of air conditioners would go up along with the temperature.

"You know, you're right! I'll sure as hell be in town all summer, because this place is going to cost me my vacation pay. And I hate the heat! An air conditioner will save my life."

Make it a lot livelier, too.

We talked of pictures and agreed to frame the two dark Chinese scrolls in bright modern brass. We agreed that most women would love to own a Renoir, a Degas, and a Monet. We also agreed that many of them have wound up with those oil paintings of thyroid-eyed, scurvy-ridden children. Or scenes of Paris in the rain. Or Paris in the sun.

Buying wall art is as easy as buying picture-hanging hooks. Many times, the picture-hanging hooks look a lot better than the art they suspend.

What to do? Look for good graphics. Posters have reached a new height in looks. Lithographs in black-and-white, or with color, are available in quantity. Often by famous artists. They are inexpensive, unless you're trying to get signed ones in limited editions.

Go to small art shows. To neighborhood fairs, money-raising events, even art schools. Visit the best museums in your city. Look at the best; then buy what you like.

Buy books on art. There are some huge old ones available at

discount bookshops. Some of the prints in them are handsome enough to frame.

She was in love with Picasso's classic period, Chagall's lovers floating in clouds, blueprints of ship designs, John Marin's odd watercolors of the sea, pictures of costumes harking back to—almost to the fig leaf.

When we got them (the toughest to find might be the ships' blueprints), we'd frame them all at once. If that's possible, it's best. Framing costs can go down with quantity orders. I follow a very simple rule (if I'm not dealing with a very valuable original): frame fancy pictures simply; frame stark, simple subjects more fancifully.

We'd use her entry hall as a gallery; our ceiling fixture would be a series of spotlights on a single, central strip, the lighting aimed at the picture walls. None hitting you in the eye. (You can readjust their angles easily.) Any good lighting-fixture store has variations on this type of fixture. The prices vary, too; you don't need the expensive ones to achieve the effect.

Just as I was mentally patting myself on the back for having set most of my "male snares" without her being aware of it, she said, "What about the bathroom? I thought you decorators were crazy about doing up bathrooms!"

Some are. I'm not. No matter whose bathroom I'm "doing," I start with the premise that a bathroom is the place you go when you're suddenly sick. One shouldn't have to worry about ruining flocked-velvet wallpaper, getting more nauseated from watching jeweled mermaids swim around the walls, or damaging the wall-to-wall carpeting.

The bathroom in the husband-angler's apartment is a real challenge.

We walked into her bathroom together. It was small but modern. All new, because it had recently been renovated. The brand-new tile gleamed pale peach. "Yuck!" she said.

A good description. The bathtub, sink, and toilet bowl matched, but the floor fortunately was white.

"A friend of mine has tiles this same color and she used a pink wallpaper with different-color sea shells on it. Some fishes, too, I think. Her shower curtain is kind of salmon color. What do you think?" she asked, looking vaguely sickish.

"What *you* need is something to tone down that peach tile. How about fake marble wallpaper—black and white and beige. Or the kind that looks like tortoise shell. Then black taffeta shower curtains—two—one on each end of the shower rod. We'll line them with standard pink plastic shower sheets." (I plunged ahead as she sat on the tub's edge with her eyes getting larger than the sink. Either she liked it or she was in shock.)

"Then we can get a set of glass shelves and put all your good colognes and bath oils on it. And the towels—no problem—all big, thick, and white. No fingertippy ones; you know what a frustration they are. And we'll add an extra towel rack down low—to hang magazines on! You just open the magazine and slip it over the towel rack sideways. And, on the floor, a fake fur rug in black and white—washable, fluffy, and you won't have to worry about bath powder showing."

What I'd done was describe a sensual bathroom, a far cry from feminine. Because young attractive women don't have to spend much time in their bathrooms applying globs of make-up and soaking off dry skin. They are just naturally beautiful.

As with all natural beauties and truly attractive women, she had enough emollients, unguents, pills, rubs, oils, make-ups, and nail lacquers to fill two medicine chests and a U-Haul.

So, to help her achieve an inspectable medicine chest, I suggested she use the low chest we were going to buy for her dressing room for some of the things that were about to burst the bathroom cabinet.

The Husband-Angler

Guests sometimes inspect medicine chests. Especially men guests. All that should remain in the medicine cabinet in her bathroom were the fundamentals. Aspirin, mouthwash and related items, and a few cosmetics.

She was not to seem to be a hypochondriac. (Except in the top drawer of her future dressing-room chest, which would hold enough medicine to stock an infirmary.)

She should appear to have natural, untinted, and curly hair. (Except in the second drawer of that dressing-room chest, where she would have enough bottles, rollers, and sprays to dye and set a sheepdog.)

And while I was helping her sort out the oddments I suggested that one bottle of good men's cologne be put on an open glass shelf in the bathroom. And the room deodorant spray that women guests always search for. (We live in an era of obsession about odors.)

And how did she take all this—at least the parts I'd actually *told* her?

She said, "Okay, the peach tile won't show up and the jars won't fall out of the medicine cabinet every time I open it."

With a little less effort than it would take to build a small ship from one of the blueprints she'd found, we were done with her apartment. Late summer.

I was invited over to share a casserole. (She'd been practicing cooking and done some entertaining; she hadn't waited until the place was finished. Waiting would have been a mistake for her or for anyone else, for that matter.)

The entry hall was a dazzler: the kitchen vista, the open bar, the spotlighted pictures and the white woodwork against the brown walls, the glass hall table holding white china serving pieces. It was an immediate entertainment.

The living room made you want to look around, because the round glass table was set; the modern chandelier suspended above it was of white plexiglass, looking like a small series of stalactites. Soft light reflected off the brass curtain poles on which the black-and-white toile draperies were shut against the night. Around the table were very contemporary curved chairs of black lacquer with added seat cushions in a bright-Mexican-pink fabric.

The captains' chests at the far end of the room held the huge sky-blue lamp. It had a big shade of white paper (opaque, remember?). You kept looking because the old dark wood glistened; the two Chinese panels above it made you think of long-ago travels. It was evocative.

The mirror hung between the two windows reflected the couch-niche wall. On that big white couch were two big corduroy-velvet cushions and a throw blanket. All in bright pinks, sky blues, and black. The felt-covered table was pale pink. Its lamp looked like crackled white Chinese porcelain. There was a huge brass ashtray. The other, a black marble table, had a differently shaped white porcelain lamp; it showed off her silver cigarette box. The matching lampshades lit a very large painting over the couch: to some it would be a sea in summer, to others drifting colors. It was an oil painting she had bought from a young student.

Her tray stand was black lacquer. On it was a large brass tray holding the cut-glass bowl. Filled with wrapped candies. It said welcome.

The bookcase was filled, too. Where spaces were left, there were the small objects she had collected. Across the top of the whole bookcase were plants. Several good artificial ferns, but among them were real philodendrons. She would care for growing things. But she'd never be a fanatic plant worrier.

The mocha-brown room was warm but cool from her window air conditioner. Angled in front of that practical window was a huge fan chair made of white wicker. Sexy, because it would make a woman feel as if she were starring in a Humphrey Bogart movie and make a man feel as if he were a *new* Bogart. It was glamorous.

The high white ceiling caught pools of light. The room had dim areas; a few large floor cushions on the brown carpet were zip-covered in the black-and-white toile. There was quiet ease.

The place smelled of bath oil and perfume, of food and brewing coffee. She cared for herself and her guests.

As she served me, she said she'd been having lots of guests from the office.

Married men?

Why, of course. Married men have something. Married men have wives, and wives are the greatest matchmakers. The wives were bringing their brothers, cousins, uncles—bachelors.

She talked of learning to ski come winter. She told me she was trying to perfect her beef bourguignon. And the secret, she said, was to keep pouring in the burgundy.

She was wearing a long orange silk pajama thing. She looked different. Unstrained. Calm. Totally feminine, but completely secure.

And her telephone kept ringing! She seemed to have become a giggler and a whisperer. And half the bottle of men's cologne in the bathroom was missing.

She finally joined me at the table and said, languorously, and perhaps showing off slightly, "I owe it all to my tuna-fish casserole."

6

The Vacation-House Schizophrenic

"It's Friday."

"Kind of you to remind me. But I had an idea it was Friday." I was on the phone, talking to an old client who seemed to sound a lot older than her years. Almost senile. Anyway, something was very wrong.

"Listen to me, Duvie, you may be the world's busiest decorator, and tired all the time. But you don't know the meaning of the word tired. Friday afternoon to me is—is—the beginning of the weekend."

So? Friday afternoon means the beginning of the weekend to at least half the civilized world, and most of the world's occupants greet Friday with a kind of glee left over from childhood memories. "Hooray, no school tomorrow or the next day!" At least I do.

But she continued to sound more and more as if she'd been recently disinterred. "We go to our summer house for the weekend. We haul things, not counting the children, who seem to have multiplied. We get out there in time to greet guests. I spend the whole weekend cooking, cleaning, loathing it, screaming, scrubbing. And for *this* I've waited most of my life. What a ghastly waste."

128

The Vacation-House Schizophrenic

If you've waited most of your life for a second house—the vacation spot—and it's driving you crazy, it would seem to me the thing to do is fix it up, fast.

"Connie," I asked her, "why don't you fix the place up some, so it's easier to handle?"

"Because I *hate* the place. We've had it for two years now and it's not getting *any* better."

Now, I happened to know that they had ransacked newspapers, magazines, maps, and the brains of a dozen real-estate agents before they'd bought the house. The trips they'd taken just to inspect it would have equaled the mileage on a used spacecraft. And when they'd first told me about it, they had *talked* of improving it.

No house can get better by itself. The trouble with a second house is usually the offhand treatment it gets. Somehow, it's supposed to be ready for you when you get to it because it's your own personal resort. To be realistic, if it's to be ready for *you*, you've got to give *it* the same amount of thought and work that goes into planning a small commercial resort hotel.

My exhausted friend on the other end of the phone didn't need to be told that she must have overlooked a few things or made a few mistakes. She knew it. But she had to be pulled out of a hole before she drove herself into a neatly dug rectangle.

"Listen, Connie," I said, "why don't you stay home this weekend and just let Sam and the kids go?"

"What would they *do* without me?"

"Manage."

"The hell they would. And Sam would never speak to me again . . . and my garden . . . and . . ."

I couldn't cajole her into staying home. Instead, *I* was urged into coming out.

If you are not happy with your home away from home and if you don't happen to have a decorator friend who is a vacation-house buff, then hire one. Because your long-awaited vacation house needs help if it's a constant source of agony. Maybe you'll need an architect to redo some of it. But an architect is not a decorator—and, I assure you, the reverse is also true. (Architects are in love with the walls decorators always want to remove. Or they'd like the whole place left barren so that you see the masonry, or something.) Anyway, you're going to need some professional help. And most of it may have to begin with your banker, stockbroker, or pawnbroker—any source of money you can attack.

In order to reach a holiday house for the weekend, one surely needs to travel. I always try *not* to travel with the friends whose place it is I'm visiting. I like to be picked up at the station and come upon the house as any guest would. Also, I don't want to be in any conveyance that has the usual weekend haulage in it.

Some of the haulage *is* necessary. You can't have a spare set of children, one for the city, and one for the country. But is it not possible to own two, or possibly three, toilet plungers, raincoats, umbrellas, broken stepladders, can openers, brooms, quart jars of peanut butter?

A cardinal rule for weekend householders should be that each member of the family may travel with only *one* small suitcase or duffel bag. What he puts in it is his own business—unless he's under ten or is a dog, cat, or goldfish. It's amazing the amount of surviving that can go on with just a minimum of luggage.

If your vacation home is anywhere within the existing hemispheres, reachable by public and private roads, considered habitable and taxable by county agencies, there are stores, hospitals, neighbors, constabulary, and drive-in movies nearby. You need not starve, go without Band-Aids, or die for lack of recreation because you forgot to bring something.

It is taken for granted, of course, that all vacation areas spawn crooks. The groceries and services—all the necessities of human

The Vacation-House Schizophrenic

life are supposed to be costly, costlier, and costliest in remote spots. But aside from the fact that all these needs had to be installed or hauled to those distant spots by the people who sell or perform them, it's worth more to lug less. Pay more, if necessary, or stay home. You'll be happier.

For instance, when I went to visit my friends' house, Sam picked me up at the station and said he had a "few stops to make" en route.

"Would you believe it," he said, "we got out here with *every-thing*—except we didn't have one blazing thing to eat for dinner!"

We finally reached the house at dark. And drove circuitously around to the back. Whatever happened to the front doors of country houses? Only once in all my years of being a semi-pro houseguest have I entered a vacation house through the front door.

We went in, and we were in the kitchen. This was the kitchen I'd been told about when they'd bought the house. I distinctly remember Connie having said to me, "Finally, Duvie, I've got a large kitchen. I mean space. Early American, Early American —I'm going to have it all Early American."

And, boy, that's what she had.

Daniel Boone's wife had a more workable setup.

The first consideration in the second-house vacation retreat should be the kitchen. This is the room where most of the troubles begin. (If my friends had had a large freezer, a good oven, and reachable storage areas, dinner could have been ready shortly after they'd arrived.)

But then again, there is a form of insanity called "fresh-vege-tables-in-the-country." Perfectly sane people hit the country-side and become fresh-corn freaks. The wild dash for purchase before the little man down the road closes. The frenzied husking, the fast toss into boiling water, and the maniacal eating. All by folks who are on no-calorie diets at home and whose kids wear braces.

It is better to put off the fresh-vegetable routine until the second day out. The approach to the weekend should be handled with as much care as a minuet. Because if you start out exhausted there is every reason to believe you are going to stay that way. Or get worse.

When we were finally ensconced in their so-called kitchen, sitting around a table, eating things out of boxes, bags, and boiling pots, I had a chance to take a good look around. The entire kitchen was made up of discards. Not one piece of equipment was anything anyone would *buy*.

After dinner, I was shown around the house. At some stage in somebody's life, this had been a permanent home. In other words, a farmhouse with a basement, an attic, and rooms in between. What the sizes of the original rooms had been would have been impossible to figure out. Alterations with altercations had been happening on these premises for years. The final result was shambles.

But the house had possibilities: it was standing, it had land around it, and they owned it.

Besides, it had a fireplace, a huge kitchen area, a dining room, and a bathroom. I mention this particular assortment because they proved that the house was habitable and improvable. Having a fireplace means you can get warm. (It also means you can tell your friends you have a fireplace.) The existence of a bathroom means there is water available and some plumbing intact. A dining room can be used as an extra room or as a dining room, in case the huge kitchen area is better avoided.

There was a staircase. The staircases in vacation houses usually either are rickety or have loose banisters. In some newly designed vacation houses they are so unique they are frightening. (People who fear stepping onto a curb find themselves trying to navigate free-form spirals. Whereas those who would not let their children step into a manned elevator unaccompanied by a keeper will let those same darlings dare ancient loose treads while clinging to detached railings.)

Look out for unsafe stairs. You must fix them *immediately*. While awaiting the carpenter, put carpeting on the stairs themselves. Do something quickly about the loose banisters or stair rails. If you *can't* do anything permanent, quickly put up heavy ropes along the railings or up against the wall. And the temporary carpeting? It's something soft to fall down on. It's okay to carpet just the tread with cheap stuff precut to fit any standard stair tread. Lumpy carpeting poorly installed on a staircase is a booby trap. If all this sounds frightening, I'm sorry, but it's better to face the care or cost now than the cast later.

Ten minutes after tour time, I had Sam fixing the swaying banisters. Then, clinging to the wall, I got to the top of the stairs to see the upstairs rooms. Many, many rooms. A confusion of them, sometimes separated by a wandering hall, at other times by a connecting door. At one point, the hall itself disappeared and we went straight through one bed-strewn area into another.

Sam, in between hammer blows, called up to Connie, "Show Duvie *our* bedroom, sweetheart."

She gritted her teeth. Naturally, their bedroom was the largest; it was, however, the one you walked through after you lost the disappearing hall. In order to reach the back bedrooms, you *had* to walk through their room.

"Sam says this is our contribution to population control."

(The master bedroom, as it is so whimsically called, does not necessarily have to be the biggest. But it certainly should be the most private.)

I was shown my room. Their guest room. I believe it had become the guest room because none of the kids would take it.

Connie said she'd thought I'd be comfortable in it because it was more remote from the household traffic noises. It was also farthest from the one bathroom.

One might assume that all would be quiet and snug, because the children were tucked in for the night in their various pigeonholes. It would be an assumption only, for, despite the traveling, the smaller family members were not knocked out at all. They were busily engaged in trying to knock each other out. Country living seems to lead to country fighting. Freer. More open. Noisier. These kids liked the country: here they were able to holler unencumbered by close neighbors.

Finally, with everyone calmed down, Sam, Connie, and I were seated in front of their fireplace, waiting for the fire to roar. Which it wasn't going to do. Because the chimney was in need of repair and the draft wasn't so good. Or the draft was too good. Anyway, the only thing that was burning was Sam.

Connie was angry, too.

I suppose I should have wisely, carefully, crawled up the stairs to bed and tended to my own business. But instead I said, "You know? I think you two ought to get divorced, get rid of all your rotten kids—and, of course, this house has *got* to go."

"That's *just* what we wanted to talk to you about!"

Since I'm neither a divorce lawyer, real-estate agent, nor scout for an adoption service, I gathered they wanted to talk about something constructive. Such as the construction of their house, or, in this instance, the reconstruction.

What *can* we do with this place?"

"First, you have to be sure you really want it."

They were sure. Why? Connie was crazy about gardening and couldn't wait till daylight so she could show me her dwarf tomatoes. Sam was slowly becoming an ardent bird watcher and fisherman. The kids were swimming well and saving up to buy a small boat. I gathered there was a lake nearby.

There has to be a *reason* for a country house. Just to get away from the city is not enough. You must be going to something special.

"All right, you've all become happy outdoorsmen. Then all we've got to do is make the indoors bearable."

Connie was dying to talk about furniture.

Sam was dying to talk about construction faults.

Each of them had a real problem. Yet because part-time living is done in parts, I had to think impartially. Construction faults should be attended to first, but since they were going to have to live through the alterations *while* vacationing, we had to try to do everything at the same time.

Sam would try to get a nearby building contractor to come over as quickly as possible. The contractor would know the availability of workmen and their schedules. No matter how wisely you might try to arrange it, you aren't going to get speedy last-minute renovations in a resort area.

A local contractor could tell Sam which parts of the house needed the most immediate attention. *I* might want to redo the kitchen first, but that faulty chimney and those loose stairs might be much more important for the survival of the house. And those in it.

Of course the contractor should inspect the whole house— and he'd be the one to know a local architect, if one was needed. It was too bad that we had to rule out the handyman who had done some odd jobs for them when they first came out. His reputation had filtered down to them through some women Connie had met at the nearest shopping center. The ladies had raved about him. But, like any man with too many mistresses, he'd gotten overtired and undependable. Sam and Connie showed me a neatly drilled hole in the kitchen wall. The empty

The Not So Terrible Move

hole was waiting for a piece of pipe to connect to an outdoor shower. The shower parts were in parts unknown. As was the handyman.

We discussed procedures. Then Sam went off to bed; he and a particular bird had a dawn appointment.

Connie leaned back and said to me, "Why do I hate the inside of this place so?"

"Connie, remember when we did your place in town? Remember all the furniture you couldn't wait to get rid of? Are you aware that this place is *entirely* furnished with the furniture you loathed in the city? Did you think the fresh air was going to make it look better?"

"Well, for heaven's sake, isn't that what everybody does—unless they're millionaires?"

"Yup, and it's the main reason women hate their country places. And if it's any comfort to you, millionaires sometimes do the same thing."

"All I know is—well, it was a terrible job to move it out here." Familiar words.

Now, if you're bound and determined to bring entire loads of hated furniture to your country house, at least refinish or repaint it first. Bring it out fresh. If you can't do the work in town, be sure your first houseguests like to paint furniture. (Many people do. I think they're idiotic. But maybe they'd rather paint furniture than bird-watch or rave over shrunken tomatoes. Come to think of it, I once painted a piano, complete with flowers all around it, in order to get out of going to a country fair with my hosts and a batch of kids, including my own son.)

Connie went off to the kitchen and returned with a large cracked bowl. In it were a few broken pretzels. "Here," she said, "here's to gracious living in my country house."

"Connie, if you had the chance to design a vacation house for yourself from scratch, what would you want first?"

The Vacation-House Schizophrenic

"Complete psychoanalysis."

"You can examine your own head to find out what you want in a house in the country."

From underneath a two-year accumulation of magazines and Sunday newspapers, she dragged out a battered edition of *House & Garden*.

On its cover it said "Vacation Houses." Inside, there were vacation houses. She pointed to several astonishingly beautiful photographs and looked anguished. "Look at the way these people live," she said woefully.

"What people? I don't see any people."

Decorated rooms in magazines are made to look at, not to live in. Think about it. Have you ever seen an ashtray full of cigarette butts, a semi-eaten slice of pizza on a cocktail table, any exposed light cords, one single sneaker on a chair, one unplumped pillow, one stain on a slipcover, one burn on a rug— or one filthy dog? No. The dog is either a freshly coiffed poodle or a porcelain one, and any people who may seem to appear are really choice pieces of statuary. Rooms in magazines are created to inspire you, not to make you want to expire.

Look in the back of the magazine for the sources and credits —or the shopping information. You'll see how much of the stuff you envied was borrowed, how much is not commercially available, and where you *can* get the things you really want, need, and can afford.

There is not a check-out counter at a supermarket that doesn't have a magazine designed to delight you with its marvelous decorating ideas. Use your eyes. Enjoy looking. Then use your head.

"Well," said Connie, "I guess I really want something chic, cheap, and kind of antique."

(She was mostly enchanted with places whose owners' major concern was how they were going to get away from the Mexican hacienda in time to open the London flat to meet the crated painting being flown in from the New York town house.)

What Connie was liking to the point of madness was cleverness. The expensive kind.

"Connie . . . in decorating you can be clever without going bankrupt. But clever is not putting four hundred dollars' worth of indoor tree into a busted wooden bucket—painted purple— that was a fifty-cent 'find.' " Clever (and smart) in the country house, I told her, is:

Color	Blankets	Screening
Canvas	Sleeping bags	Matched dishes
Kitchens	Rock collections	Garbage cans
Plastic	Humidifiers	Bathrooms
Foam rubber	Dehumidifiers	Air conditioning
Towels	Shell collections	Window shades

After reeling off that disparate list, I suggested we retire for the night. Connie and I entered my room and we both glanced around. She said, "Gets cold in here at night, Duvie. I'll give you some extra blankets."

The extra blankets matched the regular blankets that I had at my disposal—six large rags.

"Remember what I said about blankets being clever? . . . They are indeed a unique touch in country houses everywhere. And believe me, Connie, no matter where a vacation house is, it's nearly always either cold or damp at night. Or both."

She nodded understandingly and tiredly. Because she'd had to traverse the upstairs tundra to get me my towels and washcloth from a distant closet.

"Don't say a word about these. I've been meaning to replace them."

I couldn't. I was laughing too hard. I was supposed to dry myself with a shredded terry-cloth beach towel featuring Donald Duck. My washcloth was a lacy relic from a Tucson motel. My hand towel was half of a regulation bath towel; it had a name tag on it and a number. Camp Onoto—221.

We both sat on the bed to recuperate. But that did nothing to relieve the general hysteria. We were perched on a damp rock garden that squeaked.

"I know, Connie . . . it came with the house." The beds in the standard country house make you pray for morning. Until they can be replaced with foam-rubber mattresses—to say nothing of their Neanderthal bedsprings—wouldn't it be nice to have a dry, warm, full-size sleeping bag?

She left me in my damp bed, reading a sodden paperback by the light of an exposed 20-watt bulb poised atop a busted ceramic fish. "Well coordinated, Connie, the fish motif is perfect for sleeping underwater."

There was no problem rising Saturday morning. The sun rose inside my eyelids via my shadeless window. Several children called me to breakfast.

Adults who've spent a miserable night meet as cranks in the morning. So do children. Our immediate decision over coffee was to get new mattresses at once. Firm, very thick, foam-rubber mattresses (they survive any clime). We could hope that a carpenter would be provided by the contractor. Then the mattresses would be placed on wooden bases consisting of deep drawers to serve as storage space for room and bed user. Until that day came, the old springs would hold the new mattresses and each room was to be supplied with a footlocker. Available at Army & Navy Stores, they're cheap, neat-looking, and made to withstand muck and mire. If you're willing to spend a little more, they can be had in color. Most important, they're metal, seal shut, and, in the vacation house, would give each room its own dry linen and blanket supply in its own trunk. (Later, the footlockers can be used as night tables, or for peaceful travels.)

The Not So Terrible Move

While awaiting all this comfort, we'd sprinkle the present mattresses with scented talcum powder to absorb some of the moisture and cover the lingering smell of mildew.

If there's a town nearby with the likes of a big chain store that has national outlets—the kind that sells everything from tractors to toasters—order your vacation-house needs from them. Nearby stores with affiliates equipped to serve rural areas know what to do about orders and shipments. They can supply advice, guarantees, and service. What they don't have in stock can be ordered from catalogue.

Sam went off to locate a contractor. If he couldn't find one, I suggested church the following morning. It is not only a commendable thing to attend religious services, but that's about the only place you'll meet the locals who'll know who does what and how well. A reverend's wife will know if there's a contractor in their congregation, or at the temple in the next town. I don't care what your particular rites are, or how or if you practice them. In the country, you've got to know some of the residents. It's hard to become part of a community when you're just a "summer person". *Try* to join *something*. To live in comfortable seclusion you need local people.

After breakfast, Connie and I faced the stack of battered dishes in the battered sink in the battered kitchen. She'd been hiking twenty-five feet to put milk back in the refrigerator; that's how far it was from the sink edge where the bottle was perched. All that floor space was a woman-killer.

Your kitchen equipment is best arranged for you when it is lined up galley style. Counter space between each separate piece: next to the refrigerator, on each side of the sink, plenty on each side of the range. But sacrifice anything to have a wall oven, a refrigerator with a huge freezer and ice-cube maker, a dishwasher, and a large serving counter to back you up. You turn around from cooking and put the dishes on your serving counter. This also acts as a divider between the cooking debris and the dining debacle.

I like metal cabinets in vacation-house kitchens. Or Formica. (I am not overly fond of dark wood wall-hung kitchen cabinets, anywhere. I think they look like suspended caskets.) Spend money on your working equipment. Never mind the fancy cabinetwork. A very shallow closet, with shelves for one row of drinking glasses on each shelf, is a good-looking and practical way to cover, say, the exposed side of a refrigerator. With a glass-paned door going from floor to refrigerator top, you have glasses made easily accessible for what everyone wants to do most on vacation: drink.

Also, don't forget duplicate canned-food storage. If you've got the space, use another closet device: shelves just deep enough to hold two or three of everything, easy to reach, and providing an at-a-glance inventory. You might want to have a blackboard on this closet door. You'll be jotting notes on what you'll need next. Constantly.

Everybody knows about garbage in rural areas. You have to separate the garbage. (It is a task I find almost impossible to do correctly, anyplace.) So label the containers: "Bottles," "Cans," "Papers," "Foodstuffs," "Mulch Pile." Whatever classifications your family and guests will recognize. You'll find out the pickup days or the means available to get it all hauled away. There may be a town dump you don't know about. If so, there is also every reason to believe you'll need a permit to use it.

Connie was listening to me and watching as I made notes for her. She was folding damp clothes, in hopes of a sudden sun at noon, whereupon she'd race outdoors and hang them all up again on her clothesline. You've got to have a clothes washer and dryer if you don't want to spend your vacation life doing sun dances. I don't care if you've never washed anything more complicated than your hands in the city. In the country, laundry piles as high as an elephant's eye. And *you've* got to do it. (Taking dirty laundry back home is asking for extra luggage— and a city chore that'll make you hate *both* your houses.)

Connie glared at me over piles of raggedy clothes and linens, "If you think I'm going to risk those basement stairs in order to have clean and dry *anythings,* you're crazy."

I shall only say that their basement could have served as storage cellar for wines, home-canned goods, or chained prison- ers. Its dirt floor supported an antique heating system, a coal bin, a woodpile, and an unusual water tank. The cellar stairs were navigable by, perhaps, an octopus wearing cleats.

The laundry room shouldn't be in the basement. Not in her house, for sure. And not in any country house, for convenience.

"Connie, just think of one area of this great, big, kitchen ruin as a laundry section. Keep it well away from the cooking-eating section. Preferably near an interior door, so that dirty-laundry bearers may haul it into the laundry division without traversing the whole kitchen." (Wouldn't a laundry chute from upstairs be great? Shouldn't be too tough to arrange, considering the usual highly demolishable state of vacation-house floors and ceilings.)

We'd use the wall nearest the dining-room door for the laun- dry equipment. With a huge straw hamper for "deposits." A cabinet above for soap powders, bleaches, and everything else —including sewing supplies.

And, yes, you need an iron and an ironing board. Of course everything is wash-and-wear and drip-dry. But when you're ready to return home, your traveling clothes may still be drip- ping. Your washer-dryer may conk out and you might just need to warm up a few bed sheets in a hurry. The luxury of the iron-on patch can only be appreciated by the use of an iron.

The windows over the sink were mismatched and afforded a view of the washline. (Pretty scenery backing up a clothesline is a waste. So we'd move the clothesline to one side, and be sure we purchased a good one, with multiple arms, umbrella style.) We would hope for a big window with screens, with a low planter box on its sill. A window over a kitchen sink lets you have a visual vacation while you're doing a few cups. But *not* if the sill is full of jars of hand lotion, scouring powder, and poison-ivy spray cans. Decorate your windowsill so that there simply isn't the space *on* it for ugly things. The two other windows in the kitchen, would, we hoped, be fixed to work. Replacing them entirely was the real and sensible answer.

Oddly, resort houses are nearly always gloomy. They take on the aspect of caves. Possibly because their original tenants did not use them solely for vacationing, and wanted to feel safe from the elements or invading marauders. Anyway, the tiny sleeping rooms, the inner halls, major rooms: all of these houses must have been designed to dilate the pupils of one's eyes.

But even if you have a new all-glass house, use color, the vivid color you'd be fearful of living with in a permanent home. Because you don't live permanently in your vacation house. You can divide it up room by room. It can be a lifesaver to do each small bedroom in its own special color. With towels, blankets, sheets carrying out the same color. Then there'll be no linen-sorting problems. No fights over whose blanket is whose. (A good blanket coverage for Connie's house, which was cold and damp, would be one thermal blanket and one heavy wool blanket for each bed. Cover the thermal blanket with the woolen one for real warmth. Thermals keep you very warm only when *they* are covered. You might have noticed that thermal underwear is worn *underneath* outer garments. That's not only for modesty's sake.)

Bedspreads should be washable heavy cotton. They can all be alike. Even if the sizes vary, you might get a better price because you'll be ordering a batch in the same style, by the same manufacturer. But if you can't get a discount, still buy the very

143

best you can afford. In a heavy reversible weave, they'll last, they can be used for extra cover, and if you get a couple more than you actually need, you'll never have the unmade-bed look of the usual holiday home, even if one spread is in the laundry or has wound up on the beach.

By noontime, the sun was high; the countryside was one solid mass of greenery, flying birds and bugs, children, and food preparation. There was a dreadful undersupply of dishware and bathrooms.

What sort of clever dishes should one have for the country? Plastic ones. Melamine, or any other kind that resists stains, can go in a dishwasher, and won't show scratches. Get yourself plenty of dishes and glasses. (You'll be happy with disposable paper plates and drinking ware for approximately the length of one picnic—or one checkbook.) The silverware doesn't matter at all. As long as there's enough, and you have some sharp knives. Which can be sharpened with a no-kidding, always-on-the-premises knife sharpener—also nice for scissors, scythes, and all the other lethal weapons that make for simplistic living.

If every vacation house had a downstairs bathroom, with an entrance from *outside* the house as well as inside, there would be more peace on earth and general good will. It doesn't have to be fully equipped with a tub, but a shower is a great idea. (Entering dirt or sand bearers can be made more acceptable by having a water-hose attachment near every entrance, too.) But that extra bathroom sink, that extra toilet equipment will be the most luxurious necessities you've ever had.

With lunchtime came all sorts of problems and all sorts of additions for the house. The problems were the exhausted children and matching Mama. The additions were: rocks collected by the rock hound, shells by the shell specialists, and petrified-wood specimens by the child who collected those. "Save all that stuff, Connie," I said as she was about to dump it out midst screams and cries. "All those things, if preserved correctly, will be your unique accessories." You buy shells or mineral rock-pieces, or petrified wood in the city to liven up the décor. Why not dignify them at their source? And save money.

After lunch, Connie suggested that I see her garden. As we were falling down the front steps (I'd insisted upon seeing if the front door worked, and it did, "But about these steps! . . ."), I said to my hostess, "Amazing that human beings don't get the bends from the changes in temperature in a resort spot."

"I go from sunstroke to frostbite without so much as a whimper," she said.

"Then get an air conditioner for at least one room. A room cooled during the day is less damp at night, and an air-conditioned room can be ventilated during a rainstorm. It's especially cozy when a summer heat wave descends."

She looked at me with shock and amazement. She was part of that clean-cut, honest group who think that vacation living should be done at nature's own whim and rule. Well, you don't *have* to tell anyone you have an air-conditioned bedroom in your country home. But have one air-conditioned room. Then get another, if you and your electric current can afford it. (Until you fix the old heating system, or get a new one, you can use room heaters, but be sure they are safety-tested, guaranteed, underwritten, etc., etc.)

"And, Connie, you can get a dehumidifier for one of the big closets where you leave all your weekend clothes."

Their weekend clothing was, like most everyone else's, ready for a thrift shop. But she knew it *would* be nice to change into dungarees that didn't need wringing out, a bathing suit that wasn't predamped, or a fleece-lined coat that was immediately warming.

And a humidifier is a life preserver for those desertlike spots where everything begins to crack from dryness.

The Not So Terrible Move

Nature is grand and glorious in its own rough state—for Eagle Scouts. But they have been *trained* to survive in it. And they shop for the most modern camping equipment in order to do their surviving without overt suffering. I know all about this; my son is an Eagle Scout. And, let me tell you, Jeff may be sloppy at home, but his camping equipment gets the care usually afforded only to surgical instruments or premature babies. When he and I go to the country together to visit rusticating friends, I don't worry about a thing. What we'll need will be in his backpack: rickety staircases will be held together with his rope knots, warming fires will be built using even wet wood, and an ax will be used *correctly* to get extra wood.

If you can, raise an Eagle Scout of your own. Or borrow or hire one as a part-time counselor for your kids or husband. Buy every book on safety, fire prevention; someone's got to know first-aid and basic survival techniques. (For the times you need help and your phone or car fails, or the neighbors are away.)

We inspected the garden. Connie had raised her tomatoes without the aid of any insecticides. She wasn't getting much in the way of tomatoes, but she could have written a treatise on the proliferation of insects.

I considered the insects and said, "Connie, what about a screened porch?"

A screened porch, she thought, was a lovely idea. When you add a porch, you cut down on light source, so be sure to place it off a room that gets its light from plenty of other sources. Sit around outside your house to be sure of porch placement. There can be no rule on what's the best spot, so test it out yourself at the hours you'll use the porch most. (Almost the same thing would apply to a deck addition on a beach house. Any rooms underneath the deck will be thrown into constant shade, so that's the big consideration in placing a deck well.)

Check with the contractor on your chosen site for any addition. Then build it fast. Because it *will* change the looks of your house: and when it's new, it will usually look like a freshly applied bandage. (But remember vines can grow up on it and it'll weather and soon match the rest of the house.)

Then Connie said, "Duvie, so far, all the talk has been about constructing this or that and getting good equipment or rebuilding. It looks as if we won't have any money left for furniture!"

"You shouldn't *spend* much money for vacation furniture." Cheap is not only less costly but it will actually be better for you and your house in the long run.

I said cheap—not unattractive. She already had furniture that was worthless as well as useless. She could easily get new inexpensive furnishings that would be just as ugly and uncomfortable. Trying to emulate a manor house by using bad reproductions of antiques, or using matchstick modern for the understated getaway home, can be just as disastrous.

Sam rejoined us as we were about to have a fight about the living-room couch. It was a monster of a piece that could hold four oddly shaped children, a prone parent, a perched decorator, an overfed dog, and several large books on flowering birds and flying gardens.

Connie wanted the couch out.

I swore it was about the only thing that should stay.

"The only place that couch needs to go, Connie, is to the nearest upholsterer." Country upholsterers are cheaper than city upholsterers. (Unless you're in a very chic resort.) Look for the nearest small town; it will probably have an inexpensive upholsterer and drapery and slipcover maker. Their work is almost invariably good. This is not where you'd go for fancy tufting jobs, matched weltings, magnificently applied nailheads, slipcovers that fit like upholstery; but it is where you get practical work, proudly done, because this place has probably been serving the area for a long time and plans to continue.

"Redo the big old couch in heavy sailcloth, and have a sturdy slipcover made at the same time." The slipcover could be in a lightweight canvas. Awning-striped. There's nothing more practical than canvas in the country.

I'd changed her mind about the couch. I continued: "And, Connie, bright color—remember? Think of the room's walls being barn red with white woodwork and ceiling. Then we can have awning striped canvas of green on white—whatever's available. Use it at the windows hung on white poles—and on the couch. In fact, we could upholster the couch in the awning stripe, then have a slipcover for it in sailcloth. Say, in a light blue, like denim."

I was testing for reactions. Easing her into pattern. Feeling her out for color preference. What's appealing to the imagination—for instance, the green and white striped awning fabric —might be difficult to accept as upholstery fabric. Because upholstery implies *permanence*. The denim blue might have more acceptance for the long pull. The barn red for the walls was, of course, daring and dramatic. Another thing: strong, strong color is very wise for hacked-up walls.

The durability of the canvas got to her. It would keep out the drafts—she liked the window idea. Then, "Duvie, red walls with that denim blue, with the white woodwork—red, white, and blue! Early American!"

To say nothing of late French, current English, contemporary U.S.A.

"Okay, Connie . . . I'll bet we can get blue and white awning stripes. The entire living room can be a tribute to Betsy Ross."

Then I told her about the directors' chairs we should get. With white wooden frames and removable blue canvas covers. Foldable, durable, serviceable, and very handsome. Stools to match for putting feet up on—or for more seating.

The Vacation-House Schizophrenic

The big couch would be for slop-around comfort (the real reason for the slipcover), the chairs for no-worry seating.

The new tables should be plastic. Sleek, shiny, and white. Survivors in any kind of household. Impervious to weather and food conditions. Plastic tables are purchasable everywhere. They come in all sizes and prices. Very cheap ones are all right, but don't try to sit on them; they are not as strong as they look.

We'd stain the mismatched flooring. There were some original wide boards, but they'd been interspersed with narrow-strip patching; all would be covered with impartiality by dark, dark stain.

The big comfortable blue couch would face the big fireplace, with the director's chairs pulled up to it. On the floor of the plopping section: a large throw rug. Cotton shag. Royal blue and white, machine-washable.

"How can I wash a big throw rug in a washing machine? I'm not intending to buy a car wash."

"A large throw rug can be *two* small throw rugs, put together. Double-faced tape (it sticks on both sides) will keep the rugs together. And it anchors them to the floor without a lining. If you buy two rugs—each, say, three by six feet—they become one wedded couple of six by six. Held together, on the floor, by tape. Alone in the washing machine, by necessity."

Then we went into the dining room, where I said to Connie and Sam, "This room needs a big old round oak table. Not only for dining, but for games. No matter how great this house gets to be, it's going to have to survive rainy days with your children. They've got to be kept busy. This is the room for it and for a portable TV set." TV in the country? If you normally don't believe in television anywhere, one rainy Saturday in your rural retreat will convince you of its near magnificence.

Bold bright color in the dining room, too. Denim blue on the walls—the same blue and white striped canvas curtains as in the living room, hung by white rings on white wood poles. We'd use modern wooden chairs in a red lacquer finish with matching red seat cushions covered in washable corduroy. (All the chairs I've spoken of are available at any chair-door-table store. If there's not one of these proliferating stores in the vicinity of your country house, buy the chairs in the city and have them shipped; they're so cheap it's worth the extra cost.)

But for things to buy in the country: every locale offers something in the way of junk shops, antique shops, auctions. Here's where you look for a dining-room buffet, a big fire screen and andirons, bookcases with glass doors (because it would be nice to have books neither crisp nor limp), porcelain jugs, crocks (to make into interesting lamp bases). Get a section of wrought-iron fencing to hang on a wall as a headboard behind a bed, or on the wall just as pure decoration. Porch furniture—rockers, a porch swing, cheap chandeliers that look crazy.

Remember most of the stuff you buy will be headed for a paint job, so take a second look before you turn away. Don't worry about poor wood finishes and scratches, though be sure the drawers work and that handles or hinges can be replaced. And storage space is what you're looking for in the larger wooden pieces.

The country house is where you can use family photographs, homemade pictures of birds and scenery and pets. Frame them yourself with the easy-to-use all-plastic frames, the precut metal strip frames: all commercially available and inexpensive. Pictures must be protected from the elements. You don't need expensive framing for effect, but if you find a beautiful old frame, you can use it for a mirror.

Connie and Sam listened to what I'd been saying: color is the clever cover-up. The furniture we'd use was not expensive because it wasn't trying to be anything other than what it was: vacation furniture.

The Vacation-House Schizophrenic

Connie and Sam's children got into the act, too. Each child had decided on a color for his or her own bedroom.

They *would* get some paint-sample chips to choose from. If two kids wanted the same color, we'd let them use it. It would be cheaper and easier. If they chose wild color, we might do just one wall in it—have the rest in white. We'd use café curtains wherever possible, but we'd be sure they were full and lined in a weather-foiler fabric.

We'd put window shades in all bedroom windows. White, lightproof, laminated, and heavy-duty, they'd keep out light *and* drafts. They might have a floral motif appliquéd on them, or they could be striped, bordered, or scalloped. Using them with the completely adjustable café curtains, we could control light and weather.

At dinner we all talked about the kitchen and realized that it would be the room of most discomfort for the longest time, because it had to be the most carefully finished room in the house. I always favor all-white appliances and metal cabinets in vacation houses, because all-white and metal is the cheapest and fastest for delivery in major appliances, too.

Then we had to choose a kitchen color. I suggested mustard (because it's sunny, strong, and good with white or wood finishes).

With a color fixed in our minds, I discussed flooring-for-a-renovation. Things would be hauled in and out for a long stretch. Some portable items might be rearranged, as well. I suggested *no* permanent flooring right then. Linoleum was worth lots of consideration because it *gives* it. Many inexpensive linoleums are handsome, but they don't require lots of labor or time to install. And it wouldn't be necessary to remove sections of recently installed floor tile or carefully matched wooden flooring if a pipe went wrong. Which always happens. All that would be needed would be the removal of a strip of

The Not So Terrible Move

linoleum—then it could be replaced easily.

We could wallpaper the ceiling with something lovely (perhaps marigolds—yellow and orange, on white), because the ceiling would remain pretty much in place as everything else got done and redone. (I usually suggest ordering an extra roll of wallpaper—and always wallpaper with a vinyl coating for a kitchen ceiling.)

We'd get a long skinny table for kitchen eating. Like a harvest table. Here's where a good reproduction would be a fine idea. Narrow tables in kitchens hold less central litter, so they get cleared off more often and speedily.

One of Connie's favorite magazine clippings showed two long benches pulled up to each side of a harvest table. Each bench would seat four people. (The dining-room chairs could be used in the kitchen for emergency seating, because benches often inspire battle among kids seated too closely.)

We'd use kitchen lighting that worked on separate switches, so the cooking area could be unlit when the dining began. If there were wall-hung cabinets, lighting could be installed under them. For the ceiling, white milk-glass globes would give a bright even light.

Saturday night and bedtime arrived, and no one was offended when I reminded them that the contractor, when they had found one, should be invited to roam around in their upstairs. To decide where to put an extra bathroom and to untangle the hall.

I left early on Sunday.

Of course, there were phone calls back and forth in town and I went out a few more times.

They'd found a local contractor, who, luckily, had three sons, all of whom worked for him and wanted to stay in business.

Only one Christmas and a July 4th had passed since the renovation began when I got a phone call from Connie, saying,

The Vacation-House Schizophrenic

"Come visit the Carson place. It's done, it's great, it's a winterized summer house. We're planning to spend our whole vacation here and we even dress up for dinner on Saturdays!"

All very good signs. But I was a little puzzled. Carson, you see, is not Connie and Sam's last name.

"Duvie, it seems this place was originally owned by the Carsons, according to our neighbors. The Carsons had actually lived in it for more than fifty years. Now that we've redone it all, you'll surely be thrilled to know everyone says, 'You must go see the Carson place. We hear they're putting in an air-conditioned laundry chute!' "

7

The Retiree's Wife

Three years ago, Edna's husband, Mike, retired.

This made Edna into a retiree's wife. Which almost turned her into a raving lunatic.

You see, Mike had been looking forward to his retirement with very vocal euphoria. He couldn't understand how some of his friends had gone into that thing known as the retirement decline. *He* looked forward to doing the things he had always wanted to do. He was going to garden and build a greenhouse, and construct a workshop in the cellar. He was going to read every book on his shelves. He was going to get to know his grandchildren and the world.

He had told everyone about how he and Edna were going to travel. They were going to attend lectures and concerts. They were going to enjoy every inch of the house they had in the suburbs.

And then—he actually retired.

It wasn't two months later that Edna had made her first odd phone call to me.

"Duvie, I swear I'm going to kill him."

That was strange. *I'd* always felt that Mike would possibly murder her first. You must understand that he had always

The Retiree's Wife

seemed to me to be a happy, hale, hearty guy. *He* would make up his mind fast and pay his bills fast. All endearing qualities. *She*, on the other hand, was always complaining, always ailing; in other words, she never took the time to listen to *my* complaints.

But after several more frantic phone calls from her, I decided I'd really better see her. At *my* house. Just in case she meant what she said.

Well, if I hadn't known that Edna was to arrive at four, I wouldn't have known *who* it was dragging herself into my living room. She looked about a hundred and forty years old, all hunched over, head wrapped in a turban that seemed to be made from an old towel.

She flopped onto my couch and let out a great sigh.

Finally settled, after rearranging all the cushions, she wailed, "Look at me."

"I have been, Edna," I said. "What's the matter? You look as if you need a doctor, not a decorator."

"I just came from the doctor. *He* said all I needed was someone to have a good long talk with."

The good long talk lasted an hour. She talked about Mike. He was underfoot constantly and complained about everything constantly while doing nothing. The only thing he seemed able to do was sleep, and that he did at odd hours. Never through a whole night, but always when the cleaning woman was trying to vacuum their room. He enjoyed nothing, not even their grandchildren. Everything he'd spoken of doing, every plan he'd made, had become "ridiculous" or a waste of time. If something came up that seemed to be interesting, he'd develop a sudden cold so that he couldn't go out. But he didn't want to stay in, either. In or out, he had become unbearable.

My advice was "Edna, just kill him and get it over with. But don't botch up the job, you'll ruin the carpet."

The Not So Terrible Move

Short laughter followed by long silence. Broken by me.

"Well, what am I supposed to say . . . that you need new curtains or a lamp?"

"Funny," she said, "but I thought you *would* say something like that. Remember when I thought I was going to die from sneezing every morning? Remember, you made us switch our bedroom? And it worked?"

That was true. I'd had a feeling she was allergic to her old carpeting. Anyway, I'd installed a new nonallergenic (in her case, that had meant *not* wool) carpet in a room that faced south, painted the whole place yellow, and she'd stopped sneezing.

Maybe, this time, Mike was the one who needed a change of surroundings.

"You know something, Edna, since you say Mike doesn't want to do any of the things he was talking about—like building that greenhouse or the workshop thing in the cellar—maybe he's saying he doesn't want the whole house?"

Maybe, just maybe, the house and being around it all day was making him feel old.

It's sad to wait for a happy time and find out that it brings unhappiness. Retirement is too heralded. If it could just be eased into, then it might be the comfortable old shoe it should be.

But that weary lady needed no lecture. She wanted something definitive said to her.

"Edna, go get your hair done, pull out your summer clothes, and drag Mike and yourself down to Florida or Africa . . . anywhere it's warm. Take a vacation. Tell him *you're* feeling lousy, so that he can't turn you down. When you get back, we'll see if redoing the house might be the answer."

I would have been crazy to suggest doing *anything* to their house at that moment. An old house can be a threat to those who are suddenly feeling their years. Only getting away from it could let them know if they wanted to come back to it—to stay.

If it turned out to be just a temporary letdown, an emotional fatigue induced by the sudden change in living pattern, the vacation would be the tip-off. They would return rested and ready to start a new project.

By the time Edna left me, she was acting a little calmer. We both felt better. She had something important to do and I wouldn't have to worry about her phone calls.

One month later, she was on the phone again.

Her voice sounded all bubbly, rejuvenated, "Duvie, you darling, we want you to be the first to know—you've got a moving job!"

Their Florida vacation had been completely delightful. They were not only rested and refreshed, they were going to move to Florida permanently and had already chosen the spot. I was to give them a little hand with the move. I would have to help them decide what to take, what to leave, what to give away, and what to sell.

I went out to their present suburban house carrying the envelope file bearing their name and a lined-paper pad on which I was writing questions. I was in charge of moving a household to a house I wasn't going to see. I would undoubtedly be shown a floor plan and get hours of verbal description, because, thank heavens, *they* had seen it. It is utter insanity for anyone to buy a house unseen.

"Well," said Mike as he greeted me, "we're starting a whole new life!"

The newly sparkling Edna added quickly, "But that doesn't mean we have to throw out the whole old one."

The Not So Terrible Move

Very often there's a tendency to think that a new start can only be made if there's nothing left of the past. I think men especially feel this way.

It seemed that their new home in Florida was to be a fairly large apartment. A condominium. Which meant they owned only their own apartment and were not necessarily responsible for the plumbing system in the entire building. Not like a cooperative setup, where it would seem that each tenant is responsible for everything, including each frond of the plastic palms in the lobby. (A good real-estate agent can explain the difference to you more clearly—and a good lawyer should decipher *that* explanation.)

Mike told me of one plan available to them; they could have their whole new apartment done by a store down there for a fixed sum. It would be, he said with an air of great authority, "A total-design environment."

Edna said, "Duvie, I saw several of those total-design environs, and I just don't think they're for us. They're sort of motel impersonal, you know? I had the feeling I was being encased in plastic whorls and padded lining."

It would make sense to buy a furniture package deal if you're down to totally beat-up furniture, or if for some reason you're selling your whole old house, lock, stock, and barrel chair. But, even so, I wouldn't recommend that you depend on the whole place being done for you. You're moving into totally new territory, so don't risk being traumatized by a totally finished, totally different environment in your new home. You should be changing your life-style, yes, but you shouldn't have to feel as if you're having a complete change of life.

Mike, Edna, and I were talking in their living room. Mike was in his chair. All I asked him was "Did they have any chairs like that in any of the model rooms you saw down in Florida?"

The Retiree's Wife

"There isn't another chair like this. You know it, Duvie—you had it made for me. It's my chair."

Then he added quickly, "I don't care what *anybody* says, this chair is going to Florida with us."

Edna was seated on a beige silk damask couch. That couch was no more important to her than, say, Mike or her children or grandchildren. She had become almost the total couch researcher, *cum laude*, before that seven-foot beauty had settled down in their home. She let out one of her accomplished sighs while gently stroking a cushion.

"Okay, Edna," said Mike, "if that couch will fit in the living room down there, you can take it."

Here's a word of warning if you're moving a big piece of furniture. Check to see if it will fit into the new space. Even if you're sure you have a long wall in the new apartment's living room, you've got to be sure the furniture will fit into the elevator or can be hauled up a staircase and then into the public hallway on the floor. Then you must be sure the furniture can make the necessary turns within your own apartment to reach the room and special wall space that will eventually contain it. Who'll know? Only the superintendent or manager of the new building. You must ask him if the apartment can *receive*, as well as contain, seven-foot couches. Ask *before* you ship. A piano, a pool table, anything very bulky that can't be taken apart with some ease and reassembled the same way may prove to be nearly impossible to handle. You may have to use riggers with hoists to bring the elephantine pieces in through a large window. Yes, it *can* be done. But it's costly and you'll be better off knowing about it before you get the bill.

My about-to-move clients and I walked about their house and talked about the move. What things should go to their children, all of whom were grown, with houses of their own—and, I assumed, furnishings. But Mike and Edna were thinking about giving their children, right then, the beautiful things from their house that would have been left to their children eventually. A good idea, I think. The perfect time to give your children the things you love best is when you're going to have the time left to see them enjoyed. If you're making the big move, make the big gift at the same time.

Mike and Edna then went into the small room he'd always used for reading and doing paperwork. It was full of mismatched shelving, holding what had seemed to me the accumulated excesses of books that can pile up over a lifetime. The room had never been decorated, so I had never really looked at it. I stood at the door, waiting for the tour to proceed, listening to Edna.

"Mike, for God's sake, make up your mind about these things now. The kids aren't the least bit interested in any of it, and why should we move it with us? It's just old clutter."

Mike seemed deep in thought. All he said was "Please, Edna . . . not now."

"Duvie, you do something with him. I give up." And she left.

I walked into the room. Mike turned on lights and raised the window shades. Except for the sounds of the light switches, there was silence. I looked around.

I was surrounded by books on military history. Every volume was in order; it was the most complete collection I'd ever seen. Carefully, I pulled out one book. It was autographed by its author.

I put it back in place and sat down on a stool in order to look at Mike without falling over. I was literally swept off my feet from the impact of this jewel of a library. Acquired lovingly, tended carefully, and obviously worshiped alone.

"Mike? . . . I never knew. . . . Tell me."

"Well," and he had to clear his throat to speak, "it's what

comes of buying books when you're young and not being able to stop, I guess."

"But it's wonderful. Are they catalogued?"

"You mean you *like* them?" He could see that he had met a fellow-worshiper. (No, I'm not a military-history worshiper; but I'm a *collector*. The avid collector of perfect cabbages will rejoice upon meeting the owner of a matched set of perfect turnips.)

Why would Edna want him to get rid of these books he treasured?

I didn't have to ask him; he began to tell me. His eyes weren't so good anymore; he'd read them, they took up space, they'd be hard to ship. So, knowing their value, he'd talked with several book dealers, who said they'd be very interested in seeing what he had. He'd also talked to a nearby college about making them available to their library, and they wanted to come and see the books. He hadn't called them back. Edna had watched these attempts to sell or get rid of the books, and she knew their children weren't interested in them. All she really wanted, it seemed to me, was a definite decision from Mike.

"Mike, do you need money badly?"

"No."

"You love these books?"

"Of course, but, hell, my eyes are so bum I haven't even finished cataloguing them. I just come in here every day and check to see if they're still here, I guess."

Having fooled Edna into thinking he wanted to get rid of them, having acted as if he wanted everything new, he had blinded himself. He may have had rotten eyesight, but the worst kind of blindness is not being able to look at yourself honestly.

"Mike, you take them with you. *All* of them. Books don't take away more than one foot of actual floor space when they're on shelves. They don't cost so much to ship by parcel post. You keep them with you."

He marched out of the room with me following. Whatever would happen next, I knew one thing: I had told him what he wanted to hear. Even if he never finished cataloguing them, even if he never read one of them again, the idea of having them near him, to touch, to smell their bindings, was enough.

What happened? Mike told Edna he wanted to take the books because he wanted them. Edna said okay. (Neither of them seemed to be hurt by their children having turned down the gift of the small library, though it would have been so simple if the children had taken it and Mike could have felt they were being cared for by those he loved. But I guess if you're gracious enough to give, you've got to be gracious enough to accept turndowns.)

Mike and Edna began to tell me about the local real-estate agent in charge of disposing of their old house. He'd told them to include their carpeting and draperies as part of the selling price. Not to charge extra for any custom built-ins. Wise man. Too many house sales are lost because of the *try* for extra money for things new tenants may not even want and that might be foolish to move anyway.

It's difficult not to get upset when future tenants don't like the things you love. Your light fixtures may enchant you, but not the would-be house purchaser. If truly valuable pieces are in question, and if you can't move them to the new place, you may be better off giving them to a recognized charity for a tax deduction. It's often wiser than selling them. And a lot smarter than crying over them.

If you're selling, you may have to throw in some more things for a better deal. But other items you haven't even thought about may be bought quickly. Porch furniture, lawn or garden equipment, that big freezer in the basement. It all evens out in the long run, especially if you're in the hands of an experienced, practical real-estate agent.

I'm all for taking with you beautiful chandeliers, lovely mirrors, beloved pictures. There's not a house or an apartment anywhere that won't hold or embrace any of these. Big mirrors covering small walls are elegant. A large chandelier hung low over a smaller dining table than you've had is an enchanting centerpiece. A beautiful painting rehung on a new wall is just as lovely as it was before it was moved. Certainly handsome lamps will light up anyplace.

But then we had to talk of the kind of lives Edna and Mike were going to live. We couldn't get down to the real planning until we all agreed on what their living pattern would be. We already knew what their accessories would be, what possessions they couldn't live without, but in this kind of move one must carefully assess what they must have to begin new lives comfortably.

They had chosen to live in a small town that was an extension of a long strip of resort area and not a place made up entirely of senior citizens.

"There are plenty of retirees and older folks, but there are lots of younger people, too. We never had friends who were only our age before, so we can't fit into that mold comfortably now."

Mike had given the best and most succinct reason I've ever heard for not choosing a colony catering only to the mature transplant.

"Actually," Mike added, "I think the reason I got so damned unhappy and sick *here* was because I was the only guy in the neighborhood who wasn't going to work every morning. Sure, I wanted to garden—even to build a greenhouse. But I couldn't start a garden *or* a greenhouse till it got warm. Hell, it's warm all the time down there. In *this* house, in this familiar place

. . . I was getting old. Dammit, I'm not ready for that yet!"

I wondered where he was going to garden in an apartment. Well, it turned out they would have a small terrace. But, more important, he was looking at a nearby orange grove with an eye to making a small investment. He had investigated studying real estate and was going to try to pass the necessary tests. An old friend was down there busily putting together a shopping mall. Anyway, with all this in his mind, he'd work from the new apartment for a while.

It was great that he had a new lease on life, but until he had a lease on a new office we'd have to prepare an office at home for him.

They'd have the room. Before we turned their second bedroom into the standard den and guest room for visiting children and grandchildren, we were going to make specific plans for its being a functioning office.

Number-one item: a telephone. Not a phone with two lines coming in, or an extension phone in his office, but a private office phone just for him. The simple installation of a private telephone can turn a birdcage into an office. And I reminded Edna that meant she'd have an uncluttered home-phone life of her own, too.

Besides a phone of its own, the home office, whether in a new place or injected into an old one, needs several other things.

A desk: a new desk, perhaps made of two small filing cabinets to be used as bases connecting a top of any length desired. A filing cabinet is deep, so the desk top, be it wood or a plastic laminate, will have plenty of surface space, even if it can't be very long. (Be sure there's enough room under the desk for knee space.) This whole setup is not only practical—because it can, if necessary, be moved easily to a real office—but it stores papers efficiently and can be easily rearranged within the room.

A small attractive swivel desk chair: an office-type one in a bright color, with a low back so it doesn't loom up with a "nine-to-five" look.

A desk lamp: it doesn't have to look businesslike, but a good desk lamp throws light downward. You can achieve this by using almost any kind of fairly tall lamp, but the lampshade needs to flare broadly at its base, casting a big pool of light onto the desk top.

Mike's office would be functional with these beginnings—and decorative as well, because the usual office bookcases would be filled with the books he treasured.

Mike liked the idea of modern furniture for his office. Edna said, "Mike, choose whatever you want. Duvie can help you shop for it here."

I said, "Nothing doing! Don't ship this kind of stuff long-distance. It can be bought anywhere. When you get the new telephones, they'll be accompanied by phone books with classified pages. Just look under 'Office Equipment.' Go from there."

Mike left on several errands having to do with disposing of property. A permanent move should be made with all due deliberation. As I said, don't hold out so long you lose out, but don't work so fast to get moving that you spend future time saying, "I shouldn't have done it that way. I could have made more. It should have cost us less. . . ."

But always keep in mind that you wouldn't be making a big move if everything had been so wonderful before you made it. So make your mistakes with ease and relax into a new life with its own set of fresh errors.

When Edna and I were alone, I took out my pad and pencil and started asking questions. Always write down every question that comes to your mind when you're preparing to move. You'll not only feel efficient, but you'll protect yourself from errors. Like hauling bed linens that won't fit the new beds. Or forgetting that you may really need lots of pots and pans, because you will still be eating no matter where you live, and two people eating two vegetables and a small chicken need the same number of pots that would be needed if six people were going to be served. Give a lot of thought to cooking equipment. It's foolish to spend money for two new pots because you threw away three. (Pots get stored away easily; they don't have to look good, just cook good.)

The bedroom? Edna and I looked at their old bedroom. (Everything had now become "old" in our conversations, which is actually a wise thing; it would make it easier to face leaving the homestead.)

"We need a new mattress for our bed. Maybe we ought to get twin beds now, anyway. Then we could give the kids our room when they come and use the den for ourselves . . . or get cots . . . or something."

If you've always slept together, this is not the time to change. When the kids come to stay, *they* can make the adjustments to the new sleeping arrangements. They'll be vacationing. You'll be living in your new permanent home.

I inspected their old double bed. It had a tufted-fabric headboard that matched its well-worn bedspread. We decided to order a double box spring and mattress here and soon, so that it would be there when they arrived. We'd have to arrange for it to be "held for arrival." (You must have a comfortable bed ready for you. One that you've *tried* in the showroom.)

I said, "Edna, forget about headboard-hunting for now. Your whole decorating feeling may change. You can get a headboard down there and you may really want something very different —or maybe none at all."

Keeping the same-size bed meant that their bed linens would fit. They would take blankets even to a tropical climate. You can always remove a blanket if you're too warm, but you can be chilled even in a warm climate if you have disposed of too many blankets. Besides, visiting sleepers use blankets, too.

Don't take whole matched bedroom outfits of furnishings.

Concentrate on one handsome storage piece. You may have it painted or refinished when you've finally got it in place. And now's the time to throw out clothes—those-bottom-of-the-drawer layers you haven't used in years. So one large enough chest from the bedroom may serve you both very well. (You may find eventually that you'll want an odd-size new chest to use at the bedside, which will give you extra space if you need it.)

If you've got a pretty lady's desk, take it. It can be put in the bedroom, the living room, the entry hall. Nicely shaped small desks are hard to find.

Said Edna, "You mean you wrote about my little desk on that paper pad you're always using? What's so important about my having a desk? I don't think I've used that one more than twice in my life."

"Edna, remember that Mike's going to be working at home. And if he's going to be doing that for a while, *you* are going to be in the way sometimes. A man working at home can be as bad as a man suffering from not working. So now *you've* got to have someplace private of your own—to work. You'll be writing letters, to say nothing of writing checks to a whole new fleet of workmen and stores."

Then I decided to ask her: "Listen, Edna, when you get done decorating, what are you going to do with yourself down there?"

There was a long pause. "Keep house, I guess. . . . Entertain?"

Entertaining is pretty much an extension of keeping house. In order to entertain in a brand-new house in a brand-new section of the country, or even in a brand-new mood, you'll need to know people.

The Not So Terrible Move

From having watched and worked with women who've entered the state of being the new retiree's wife, I can only warn that she must become a new kind of wife. If working at home becomes a permanent project for him, she must be busy not only at home but outside it. If Romeo and Juliet had survived, even *they* couldn't have stayed happy being together twenty-four hours a day.

How many couples live together all day and all night?

So I had another question for Edna, one that didn't come from my lined-paper pad: "Did you ever have a job?"

"No," she answered, looking a little startled. "I married Mike right after high school and then started raising a family and keeping house."

"If you had gone on to college or anything, what would you have *liked* to do? I mean, aside from being a wife, what did you want to be when you grew up?"

She thought a bit and then she answered, carefully, "I don't know what I want to be when I grow up!"

"Edna, that's good. It means you're still open for ideas. You're still thinking young."

It's a little bit of magic left over from childhood if one can still have the "wonder what I want to be or want to do" feeling.

Now was the time for her to find out.

"And think of it, Edna, you don't *have* to earn a living. So you can be as choosy as you like. If, by some chance, you do earn a couple of bucks, imagine how tickled you'll be."

No, I don't think *every* woman has to work.

But *no* woman should be bored to death. Or lonely.

Now was the time this couple had to live together: separately. As a decorator, I could help them achieve this with the private work spaces and phone setups. But no one can tell a woman she must become a professional bread baker, or weave macramé rugs, or trim neighbors' poodles, or take a course in yoga. *She* must know she wants to be active.

And an active head is just as good as an active body. If not better.

So next on the list of what to take?

"Edna, as long as Mike's taking his library, how about some of the books I've rearranged for years on *your* living-room bookcases?"

She decided to look at the shelves. "You know?" she said in faintly voiced astonishment, "I never had the time—or took the time, I guess—to read this one . . . or *that* one."

If Edna became an avid reader, she might become an avid book purchaser. Or she'd find a nearby library. And she'd meet other people who read. Something she'd read might prove so fascinating that she'd pursue it as a hobby, take a course in it: *make* a job for herself.

When you move books, take the ones you love and want to read. Forget the matched sets you bought simply because the bindings were beautiful. Or the multi-volume encyclopedia. Unless you plan to use them.

Their books would afford them each a separate library. Mike's treasures in his den. Edna's in their bedroom, perhaps. Or in the new living room. Bookcases don't have to be custom made or built-in, but in a condominium or cooperative, remember you are building for yourself as you would in a private home. So do the best you can afford. The choices of ready-made bookcases are as varied as the books you might choose. Chrome and glass, brass and glass, wrought iron (heavyweight only), combinations of metal with wood, or splendidly designed beautiful wooden ones. Books, well placed, enliven *any* room; I can't imagine a home without them.

We left the bookshelves and sat down for a cup of coffee.

"Dishes!" said Edna. "I've got enough dishes to stock a chain of cafeterias."

Give lots of thought to dishes. Even if you're giving your fine china service to your children, you may very well want to keep parts of it for yourself. For instance, the luncheon or dessert plates that you can use for buffets. Surely you'll need a couple of large platters and a big covered tureen for that kind of informal entertaining. And you'll need at least eight cups and saucers.

Set up a buffet in your head. That's how you'll know what you'll need in the way of good dishes. (Plan on eight to twelve guests.)

If you've been using mixed-up, mismatched dishes for everyday, now may be the time you'll want new ones for everyday. Why not? New place settings for the new place. For two people who like people, get a service for six. But stick to small place settings. You don't need eggcups unless you use eggcups. You don't need ramekins, small soups, or large soups; one right-size soup bowl will even serve spaghetti, or cereal, as well as soup.

If there's a set of glassware that you adore, take it. If you're not in completely passionate love with your glasses, don't take them. In the hot climates, you'll need tall glasses for iced drinks. Remember, tall glasses are often a small problem in standard dishwashers. But washing some glasses in a sink is a nice occupation. And gets the glasses clean, I've noticed. Now's the time you can throw out all the glasses from the shrimp-cocktail company, the old jelly jars, the glasses with printed-on sports cars, and usually all the residents of the top shelf in the kitchen glassware cabinet.

If you're like most people, you seem to own several hundred peculiar tablecloths. Some are so exquisite that they've only been used once, or never. And you probably have them in every size and shape conceivable. Take with you one very big, unstained, rectangular tablecloth, and take a round one. Also take one smaller rectangular cloth and one square cloth. Take at least a dozen dinner napkins. And that's enough. The *large* tablecloth will cover a rented or borrowed folding table for a party, the round one is in case you buy a round dining table, and the two others can be used on a round table, a rectangular table, or a square or bridge table. The dinner napkins are for party buffets—they really cover a lap.

Now lay out your remaining tablecloths with reverence. Let your family and friends choose what they want and need.

Your dining-table top will probably find your dinnerware framed by good-looking, wipable place mats.

Back to Edna, who was inspecting her silver.

"Take it."

"Duvie, it's a service for twelve, with every odd piece available, plus fish service and ice-cream spoons and serving pieces and . . ."

Take a silverware service for six.

Add enough spoons and dessert forks to serve twelve.

Take enough serving pieces to dish up salad, a main course, dessert, and coffee to that group you're having in for your projected buffet. (There's nothing as aggravating as not having an extra serving spoon for the salad, or an extra cake knife, or having to serve the smoked fish with the same large fork that's been spearing the sliced roast beef.)

And, of course, take everyday kitchen cutlery, including ordinary flatware for four.

If you've got one large beautiful silver tray, take it. You don't need that silver tea or coffee service, but the large tray will be useful for a batch of sandwiches on a large paper doily, or it can serve as an extra table if it's mounted on a folding stand, or it can hold a whole bar setup for a small group.

After coffee and conversation, I looked at a bathroom. It was very well appointed with about three thousand items, ranging from pin dishes and a cushioned laundry hamper to shelves wall-mounted and covered with empty bottles of cologne and enough bath powders to dust every baby's bottom in Westchester County. There were hand towels, guest towels, bath towels. Name something you can put in a bathroom and it was there. It all had to go. But not to Florida.

New bathrooms should be new. Edna and Mike would have *two* bathrooms. I'd rather they were missing an extra bedroom than an extra bath! He should no longer have to confront a faceful of stockings or underwear in order to take a morning shower. She shouldn't have to continue entering a steamed room with a raised toilet seat.

They'd have His and Hers bathrooms.

If you've just bought new towels, divide them up for each bathroom. Do each bathroom in a different color. Vinyl wallpapers with matching shower sheets and toilet seats are available in bath shops everywhere. Not only will you be stimulated by the refreshing items, you'll meet women who are busy doing the same kind of thing you are. Decorating.

Edna was a fancy bathroomer. So I told her, "Edna, now you can have a *really* fancy bathroom of your own. With those gold dolphin faucets you've always wanted!"

She was delighted. Because Edna had seen gold dolphin faucets and had wanted them for the large bathroom that she and Mike had shared. But Mike had taken a look at them in their local bath shop and had asked loudly, "Which of these goddam fish is the *hot* one?"

He'd been opposed to facing fish in the morning and he felt the same way about gilt cherub fixtures. He'd said he'd be damned if he'd grab a wing or a naked bottom in order to turn on the water.

Now that Mike had his own bathroom, he could have the

The Retiree's Wife

forty-two-way shower head he'd always yearned for, the regulation doctor's-office scale, the constantly plugged-in electric shaver, and a full medicine chest of his own.

Edna was pleased about this, too. "I'll never be accused of using his razor again," she said.

Aside from having shared a large bathroom, they had shared a large TV set. During the day, it had been Edna's, who knew the characters in every soap opera, and called other viewing friends if she missed an episode.

"Well," she said, "I guess this TV set should go into Mike's office. It'll be our den at night, so that'll mean I won't have to put it in the living room."

"Edna, you'll need a TV set of your own. If we put this one in the office-den, you'll be aching to watch it during the day, when Mike's in there."

I told her to consider having her own portable TV in the living room. That way, she could wheel it around so that it was viewable from the dining area, the kitchen, even the terrace.

She liked the idea. It would be her afternoon-TV set.

We were planning a home for two people who would meet as a relaxed couple when they *felt* like it.

I tentatively suggested they consider hiring a decorator when they got to the new town. I knew how hard it was for Edna to make decisions, and I knew that Mike would be urging her to get finished and that both of them would be adjusting to so many, many new situations.

"No," said Edna, "you're our decorator. I'll follow your suggestions and refer to your list." But then she added, "And, Duvie, I want to try to do things *for* myself, *by* myself."

Everyone probably knows a great deal more about decorating than he thinks. Anyone *can* do it on his own. Just don't be afraid of making mistakes.

The biggest mistake you or anyone else can make is waiting

for perfection. No use having empty walls while you're waiting for the perfect painting. Or not having anything to sit on while waiting for the perfect pair of chairs to put in front of the window. Living rooms have remained unlived-in because there was not the dreamed-of French Provincial armoire for the big wall. Make do, redo; but get it DONE.

No one but you will know that your home isn't finished to suit you perfectly if you don't tell them. So don't tell them.

Big mistakes only have to do with spending money unwisely. Even if you have an endless flow of money, you can have an endless flow of mistakes. Don't think having money is the answer to all decorating problems.

On my list for Edna there was a question about draping windows. She had told me they would have large glass sliding doors in the new living room, leading to the terrace. And big windows in the two bedrooms, as well. (The floor plan confirmed all this.)

Don't spend *big* money on draperies; and as for drip-dry draperies for very long window walls, whose Olympic swimming pool are you going to wash them in? And are they to drip-dry all over your floor after you've known the delight of rehanging them while they're still wet? Drip-dry fabrics are practical, of course, but for big windows don't think you're not going to have to send the curtains out to be cleaned or washed.

Smaller windows can have the wash-them-yourself curtaining. But bedroom windows should have lined or heavier fabric to keep out the light. Here's where you might use the drip-dry fabric for sheer curtaining, with lined draw draperies over them.

Most living rooms are lived in at night. But in a retirement house you'll be in there during the day, too. So don't try to open and shut massive draperies. Think airy and informally.

As I mentioned earlier, Edna's beige damask living-room couch was her greatest pride. However, she was talking to me about it as if she were taking the whole wall around it with her. It was handsomely arranged with pictures, end tables, a coffee table. Very fine-looking and impressive in its present locale. In the new place it could be oppressive.

She needed the couch. But she needed an idea that would release it and her from the old roots. I suggested a mass of tall plants to be used on one side of the couch, spotlit from the floor. (During the day, they'd get plenty of light; at night they'd look exotic.) Just one of her end tables on the other side of the couch, holding a particularly large ceramic lamp—very simple, with yellow-and-blue patterning against white. It was an old Portuguese piece and its shade was fast going into the antique category, as well. I suggested a new lampshade in beige raw silk. The suggestion almost taken, I added, "Edna, wait to see what they've got down there. You might get something you'd like even better."

Instead of talking coffee table at all, I walked her into her front hall where there was a round table with an inlaid marble top. It was tall, it held a large potted plant, and it stood, regally, under her hall chandelier. Removing the plant, I stared at the 30-inch circular marble top. All different colors, ranging from beiges to blacks, with white glimmers, and a band of bright blue marble bordering it. In its center, a kind of star in the same shimmering blue.

"Edna, would you like to have the best-looking couch-front table in Florida? Take this one."

"But it's too high."

"It's not mounted on Everest. Forget these tall legs. You can get a wooden pedestal base down there or a low heavy wrought-iron one. Just take the marble top—and have a round wooden disk cut for it to rest on, attached to the new base."

"That's marvelous!"

The hall table, lowered, would be a different piece from the one she had known it to be and would serve a necessary purpose, unusually. She would want to take her nicest small tables, but not lots of them. Because each table seems to need a lamp and a chair, which could make for crowding. An open room leads to an open feeling.

Aside from Mike's chair and her couch, we had planned to take no further living-room seating. What would be ideal in front of a big window looking out onto a terrace? A long low bench, so that one could look outdoors or inward toward the room. Since she didn't have such a bench, I told her to look for one at least six feet long. Something sleek.

"But what color?"

"When you get down there, go straight through the upholstery-fabric department of the best store in town. Buy half a yard of the material you like best."

"It'll turn out to be beige damask," she said.

"Forget that. Buy a hunk of fabric that you'd like to have a dress made out of."

"But I rarely wear dresses made of upholstery fabric," and she was smiling.

"You mean you wouldn't wear an evening dress made of beige silk damask?"

"Well, sure I would, here. But not there."

I waited for a while—because the idea was coming through. What was right and comfortable here might be uncomfortable there.

"Just see what color appeals to you most there, Edna. It might be what you'd want to cover the new bench in. Or Mike's chair. It might even give you an idea for carpeting."

If you're living in a place you own, spend money on good carpeting for the most-used floors, such as the entry and the living room. The dining area, if really separated from the living room, I don't think should be carpeted. Somebody's sure to spill something. But if you must continue your carpeting into your dining room, it must be the same top quality as your living-room carpeting. It must be cleanable. (When you shop for carpeting, ask, "How do you clean it?" Sometimes the salesman may have to suggest professional cleaning. But you'll need to know what to do for emergency stain removal. Do you use soap and water, or a special dry-cleaning compound? The store with the salesman who can answer your questions is the store you'll be safest buying carpets and rugs from.)

An inexpensive area rug would be best for any den, office, guest room. This room will be going through constant furniture changes, what with office necessities and part-time guests. And you can roll up an area rug and put it away, if necessary, for a few days. I thought I'd better straighten out the guest-sleeping problem, too. I suggested a high-riser couch. When you pull out the bottom section of one, you've got two separate single beds. Not even a large convertible sofa would serve the situation as well. Can you imagine two grandchildren sharing one large double bed? Politely? Or two visiting sisters-in-law? A high riser in handsome fabric and design is the only thing I know of, other than a bunk bed, where two who would prefer to sleep alone can sleep in close proximity comfortably.

We went back to talk of carpeting, because it can be such a trial to choose and should be ordered and installed all at once. (*After* you've shoved the furniture around, and like the arrangement.)

Bedroom carpeting should be lush-looking but not necessarily expensive, and soft under bare feet.

Carpeting in bathrooms? If you *really* want it more than anything, go ahead. But remember that bathroom floors are nearly always wet someplace. So your carpeting will be, too.

I feel the same way about kitchen carpeting. It *can* be impervious to almost everything. But if you think of how often you have to sponge up something fast in your present kitchen, then you've got to know that your kitchen carpet will always have wet spots. If you miss one spot—say, milk that soaks in and dries —you'll soon be reminded by the smell of sour milk without being able to locate the source quickly. If you're thinking about kitchen carpeting because it's easier on your feet, wear soft-soled shoes. Shoe soles are easier to dry than whole areas of carpet. Any carpet takes longer to dry than a tiled or linoleum floor. Ask the same flooring salesman about cushioned vinyl tiles, softer linoleums. And try to use the same store for all your floor-surfacing problems. It will cut down on the problems.

Edna and I looked at her old dining room. It was a formal dining room of size and grace. Its furnishings would look terrible in Florida. Edna, accustomed to the "real thing," would have a hard time adjusting to chrome and glass, or Formica, in a room that's used so much. But she would have to realize that the real thing can be real in a different way. For the new dining room, she should think of very fine terrace furniture. Wrought-iron tables with glass tops. Their chairs, too, can be as good quality and as costly as one likes. Handsomely designed bamboo, reed, wicker—all can have the permanence and elegance that make you feel at home without making you uncomfortable.

Both Edna and Mike, I said, should sit in prospective dining chairs to test them, because in their new, more sparsely furnished home, these would be the extra chairs used in the living room. And they should look as if they belonged wherever they were needed. Whatever their style, the chairs would have to be loafable and luggable.

With the terrace and its constant invitation to go out of doors, its constant view from the living room, the furnishings should be lovely, too. But whatever you do, don't buy outdoor furniture for effect alone. Trying to take a sunbath on an adorable curved wrought-iron garden seat will be more of a punishment than a pleasure. And look for outdoor pieces that can stay out-doors. Don't be a cushion-hauler, in case of rain. Spoil yourself with the luxury of a fine sprawling chaise. Woven heavyweight plastic thongs on weatherproof wrought iron is beautiful. These kinds of furnishings cost money but they're worth it. The ter-race is an extra room. (When guests come, you can bring out folding chairs, but avoid the ugly aluminum ones you'd haul to a beach. Slim, foldable chairs are readily available. They take up almost no space when stored, but in use they're easy to sit in and a delight to look at. Handy, too, for extra seating inside.)

Edna, going around with me, taking notes, showed signs of weariness. Part of it was fright, I knew—she was in for a long siege of working. She said, "And I don't even know how to start to think of how the new bedroom should look."

"Sexy," I said, "and why not? If you've always wanted a white satin and gilded bedroom, now's the time to do it. No more worrying about raising kids or eyebrows." Besides, if the plan worked, Mike would be busy doing his own work in his own place all day, Edna in hers. After dinner and a terrace drink, it would be nice to adjourn to sleeping quarters that were honey-moonish.

"Duvie, how am I going to get all these things you're dream-ing up?"

"You'll hang around department stores and shops; you'll buy because you'll *need* furniture. It'll get done because it has to be done. Just remember—when you look at model rooms in de-partment stores, notice that the ceilings are endlessly high, that there is at least one wall missing so that you can view the setup, that the walls themselves are architecturally brilliant with cabi-network or moldings or wallpaper. Notice that the simply done couch that seems reasonably priced has throw cushions hand-woven and studded with semiprecious stones. Sneak a look at the price tag on the lamp on the budget-priced English-style chest. There's every chance that you *could* buy it, but with a loan from the Bank of England."

When I left, Mike drove me to the station saying something to the effect that Edna would never get it all done. And did I think he could have a navy-blue-and-white den, or should it be brown and blue, or maybe red and blue? Stifling a laugh, I advised him to start out with the blue and see what followed.

After their house was sold, it took weeks of packing, by professional packers, before Edna and Mike were ready to move. Strangely enough, air freight proved to be a not-so-expensive way to ship bulk furnishings. And it would all arrive within the current year.

They left happily and I was glad to see them go. Because I wanted to know the end of the story. It was my own special soap opera.

Would Edna again want to kill Mike?

Would Mike kill Edna?

Could two people find happiness living together separately?

All I can say is, Edna used her desk to write me one longish letter a month after they arrived. She said she was liking blue and Mike was liking white. And she'd decided that if you lived near the sea and the sand you had a tendency to bring those colors indoors. And that the beige damask couch was being redone in blue linen to match a long bench she'd bought. And she couldn't understand how they had ever lived anywhere else.

8

The Newly Childless Household

"I am so happy I could cry."

In fact, she was crying so hard it was hard to believe she was happy.

But I was not going to waste any sympathy on her. Because we'd both just gone through the same thing: our children had graduated from high school, and had left home.

I've never understood why some people carry on about their children leaving home to go to college. Think how terrible we'd all feel if they hadn't graduated, if those ivy-covered halls were never to receive them.

I was so fed up with this other mother that I wasn't even going to answer her. Besides, I was crying, too.

So I just hung up the phone and wandered around the house, carefully, in order to avoid *his* room.

How *does* one enter the room of a recently departed child?

One can't, usually, unless the sanitation department has entered it first and made a path.

But a decorator whose child has just left home should certainly have a clearer idea of what to do with the child's ex-room.

Me? I shut the door.

Shutting the door to a room is certainly one way to get out

of having to make any decisions about what to do with its interior. But eventually all doors must open, even the door of the room of the departed child.

Meanwhile it didn't help me when the only mail that seemed to come to the house was for him. His weekly magazines, all of which I dutifully forwarded. Not expecting—and not getting—any reply. The only mail I got? Cheery notes from relatives saying something like "Well, now that he's finally gone, you can do all the things you've been wanting to do. You're free!"

Indeed I was. Free to feel miserable.

So if you're about to enter this phase, meet a few former mourners and find out how we decided what to do about the odd departures.

MOURNER NUMBER ONE:

Dinny, a friend of many years. A fellow-member of the P.T.A. A professional mother if I ever met one. Cookie baker, picker-up of other people's children from dancing school, deliverer of same to other people's doors. With two sons and one daughter, and a husband, she kept house while reading every book ever published on women's lib, men's lib, and children's freedom. I know a lot about Dinny, because, aside from the fact that our children grew up and graduated together, I was her decorator.

Dinny's daughter was always her greatest concern. She made it clear that she wanted her girl child to have every freedom, every opportunity. To be an equal in a world dominated by men. All this while sheltering her little girl in a room that began as a veritable bower. Flowered wallpaper, matching curtains, ruffles on a fourposter bed, stuffed animals; name a childish girlhood delight and it was in that room in a shade of pink.

Dinny's daughter was pretty to begin with. She began as an

adorable duckling and sailed straight ahead to swanhood. She needed her own private telephone before anyone else's daughter did.

Then the beautiful daughter decided to paint her room orange. She requested an India-print spread for her fourposter bed, which she had sprayed silver. She disconnected all the lights and lived by the glow of one spotlight aimed at a huge photograph of a rock-group star.

Dinny and I had looked at each other and the room and nodded wisely.

The summer before the long-awaited high school graduation, Dinny's daughter had announced that she was going to bicycle across the United States with a youth hostel group. More wise nodding went on. Dinny spent the summer calling me.

"Duvie, we never get even a postcard. Just one long-distance call collect from San Francisco! She'll be home in August. What should I do?"

"Put up a 'Welcome Home' sign."

"I mean, should I leave the room the way it is? You can't even focus your eyes in it. How will she be able to read a book? She's *got* to graduate, you know."

We gave some thought to the whole thing. Dinny's daughter was coming back home after being away, on her own, for the first time. Dinny saw a lot in this first return; it had to be "handled."

First, Dinny felt that her daughter must feel that nothing had been touched in her room. That any real decisions must be made by the girl herself. Not really big news, you say? All right, working together, we managed finally to decide on purchasing a little table, Turkish style, in dark wood. We put it next to the silver fourposter bed. The reading lamp for it was chosen carefully: a black china ginger jar with a pleated plastic shade. Only fifty million of these have been manufactured and sold. The total expenditure was less than dinner for four at a good drive-in.

Dinny prepared elaborately for the prodigal daughter's return. She changed the living-room furniture around. She bought enough soft drinks to quench the thirst of a desert regiment.

Then, as we shoved the living room back into original place again, she looked at me and said, "Boys are so much easier than girls."

Of course her daughter came home. She had a peeling nose, and a lot of dirty laundry in a backpack. She looked at her lamp and table and said, "Far out . . . wow! But would you mind if I painted that table white? And this orange room is knocking my retinas off. I've got to get some studying done in here this year."

By the time D.'s daughter left for college, her room was white, with walls covered by photographs she'd taken of America. And the whole room was neat. The fourposter bed had been painted black, and it was covered by a black-and-white plaid bedspread. (She had decided to study social work, and told me she wanted an orderly mind.)

I was very impressed with this whole thing. Especially when Dinny told me that the two of them had emptied the bureau drawers together, and large donations of training bras, mismatched socks, etc., had been given to a lucky charity. Empty drawers ensued. I think it was the two empty drawers that made Dinny realize that her daughter was leaving.

"Listen, Dinny," I said comfortingly, "why don't you just ask your child whether she ever plans to return home again? And would she like twin beds instead of this paint-layered, child-size fourposter. Lots of kids come home for the holidays and bring a friend from school with them. Ask her *now* if she'd like her room redone, and what kind of theme she'd like. Because *I* don't always understand what she's talking about. And I don't think you're far ahead of me."

Dinny's daughter thought the idea of twin beds was great. She'd like the black-and-white scheme continued, and she said she trusted her mother and me to make the changes.

Dinny was comforted.

We bought twin beds, put the white Turkish table with black lamp between them, and covered the beds with spreads of a black-and-white modern floral pattern. The flower-patterned bedspreads were decorator-inspired. I knew the flowers would please Dinny, and her daughter would like them because they were black and white.

We chose very simple black wrought-iron headboards for the beds. Always a good idea because they're basic and also because they can be so inexpensive. It doesn't make sense to be expensive in a room that might see lots of shifts.

Dinny wrote to her daughter often, and found that she liked using the desk in her daughter's room.

She wasn't flooded with return mail. But then, finally, came the letter announcing her daughter's impending holiday arrival. Sure enough, a guest was coming, too.

This time there was no worry about the general house being rearranged. Dinny bought the usual oversupply of soft drinks. The only additional item for the newly prepared room was extra towels for the bathroom. Dinny bought a set of pink bath towels.

Dinny's daughter arrived home looking splendid in blue jeans. So did her guest. There was only one small point of concern. The blue-jeaned houseguest was a boy.

When Dinny told me about it, all I could say was "You wasted money on the pink bath towels." Other than that, it had been a splendid vacation: her sons had doubled up, freeing one of their rooms, and the extra twin bed had been pressed into use for guitars, luggage, and visitors' coats.

Anyway, there would be other school holidays and other homecomings. And, without knowing it, Dinny had a guest room. Better than that, it was a room she herself enjoyed using.

Dinny's bouts with the changing room were proof to her, as well as to me, that a child's room must grow up, unpredictably, like the child.

In between visits, it should be usable—but it should stay somebody's special room.

When Dinny's daughter marries next spring, perhaps the room will change its color. Maybe we'll put the twin beds together with one mattress. "But, maybe we shouldn't," Dinny said. "Twin beds are easier to shove against the walls to make room for more furniture. Perhaps a crib."

MOURNER NUMBER TWO:

If ever there's been a sensible person on this earth, it's been Emily, and when her third child left for college last year, she still had two to go. No great waves of emotion were expected from her, and there weren't any.

She had developed a special technique for what she called "the constant loss of my other arm." She explained that even though she had five children, each was a part of her, though each was totally different from the other. When each child left home, it was the first and last time, again.

Having produced five children, she was aware of the fact that each one coveted something that belonged to an older one. For instance, her eldest son had worked very hard to buy a second-hand car. He had fixed it up under the envious gaze of the second son. The summer before the eldest boy left for college, the envious one had gotten his driver's license, taken a job at a filling station, and started begging to use his brother's car. The car had become a goal to him.

And Emily had watched them work out a deal, which consisted of monthly payments, perfection of maintenance, and the use of the car by the college attender on his vacations home.

An odd part of the deal consisted of care to be given to the older boy's room by his younger brother.

"Go in my room every day and count the rocks in my collection. Keep 'em clean. Don't let the other kids get at them! And paint the room green." (The green requested was the same color as the car.)

The new watchdog painted the room and kept the rocks in fine order.

So Emily picked up her technique of putting covetousness to work. Righteously.

When son number two left, *he* left behind his tropical-fish tank. His younger sister had wanted to mother those brilliantly hued "babies" for years. So, naturally, she had never been allowed near them.

This time, in return for caring for the fish tank and making him new curtains, she got the use of her older brother's room for sleep-over parties.

The room was not only in use, but lively.

Whenever someone left, he or she left behind a room and decorating assignment in return for a sought-after favor. Each room saw its own occupant come home happy. *And* a little closer to the immediate relative left in charge.

"But what will you do when the last one leaves?"

Emily looked at me and said, "Duvie, we'll always have guests and children coming home. And maybe I'll call you in to make me a large sewing room out of two bedrooms."

Good, I thought. Emily would cope.

The Not So Terrible Move

MOURNER NUMBER THREE:

Serena is a decorator's delight.

She collects rare prints, she loves special framing, she's always overjoyed with fabric changes; her idea of a great day is prowling around showrooms ogling chairs and tables, and planning new rooms. *She* should have been a decorator.

But instead I was her decorator, while she was constantly revamping her apartment, raising two kids, and being an active conservationist. Among her many talents, she has the most astonishing green thumb. You know how ugly grapefruit seeds grow? All spindly and frightened? *Her* little ones looked like lush tropical foliage ready to produce real grapefruit.

When Serena's first son left for college, she called me in. "Duvie, come help. . . . I must face the fact that his room is going to be sitting here unused most of the time."

She couldn't wait to get into that room and start decorating. I knew she must have dreamed up a marvelous idea. She probably already had fabric samples and paint chips. "Okay, Serena, what's the marvelous idea you've got?"

"I want to turn Jim's room into an indoor greenhouse!"

"Tell me, Serena, did Jim leave home for college or did he get a long jail sentence?"

"I don't think I quite understand."

"Serena, all I know is that when I last spoke to you, Jim was going to a regular college. He'll be coming home, right? Who can live in a greenhouse? If he's the same boy I remember as of last month, his socks would take root in a greenhouse!"

She reacted with apologies and astonishment.

Together we took a fresh look at her son's newly vacated room.

It was a room set up for a boy to study and play in. It had a

188

large desk with a good lamp. His bed was covered in a sturdy brown tweed and placed against a wall so that it functioned as a couch. There were filled bookcases and a brown cork wall filled with posters.

There were two low chests full of clothes, some still protruding from semi-open drawers.

There was dark brown wood flooring, covered with scatter rugs—kid's-room rugs. You know, the ones that are copies of "Stop" and "Go" signs or smile buttons—made of cotton shag.

The dark brown room had dark draperies featuring famous guns of the West. It was a fine room still, but fine for a very young boy. Not for Jim, who was now a young college student. Serena was right: it needed redecorating.

And boys *are* easier than girls. To decorate for, I mean. Because they don't keep up with current decorating and color trends the way most girls do, they're very apt just to add bits and pieces to what they have as they grow up. There may be the latest hi-fi equipment, but it will be placed on top of a large box containing the old electric trains. They hang on to their old sea shells and miniature car models as they add the latest scuba-diving equipment to the general décor. Some boys are squirrels. *Some* are neat, but a lot are not. When redoing a squirrel's room, you must keep the nut collection while bringing in the new décor.

"Serena, let's think about making this room lighter and brighter. We can get rid of the schoolboy look and make it an interesting room for a young man."

First, we chose a bright sunny-yellow wall color. We'd leave the one wall of dark brown cork. (It was not only good for contrast, but he would still be free to hang new posters on it or to keep the old ones.)

We replaced the Westward-Ho draperies with a heavy-looking woven fabric of the same bright wall yellow. I said heavy-looking. It was really a loosely woven washable linen that let the light show through. Hung with closely spaced pinch pleats, it looked nubby, rough—masculine.

We bought a ready-made couch cover in bright yellow, orange, and black. The back bolsters that leaned against the cork wall were covered in the same fabric. High style. Low price.

We changed the lampshade on the plain brass desk lamp. (It had been covered in a brownish linen.) We bought a shiny black paper lampshade. To one side of the window wall, we added a column lamp of pleated white paper that went from floor to ceiling in a kind of spiral. A cheap copy of a good one.

We got an inexpensive rug that looked like a large Mexican serape. White, black, orange, and yellow. Geometrically patterned so that it wouldn't seem to leap up off the floor.

The room was still Jim's room, with his bed, his desk. All his memorabilia from the early days were neatly packed into marked boxes and put on the top shelves of his closet, or on the new shelving we had added there. It had become a "Welcome Home" closet. In a young man's den.

And Serena said recently, "Guess what! Jim admires the room and I've got this new plant in a big clay pot, and it's becoming a tree right in front of that sunny-looking window—from the light of that crazy spiral lamp."

Plants, like children and their rooms, grow with care.

MOURNER NUMBER FOUR:

I think I'll call her Mrs. Fine. Because in order for her two children to go to college, she and her husband had to move to a small two-bedroom house to save money. They were by then missing not only two children but almost all their savings.

But Mrs. Fine said to me on our first meeting, "When I've had bad aches before, I've always gone to a doctor. As much as we believe in saving money, we believe in spending it wisely. And, most times, that takes extra guidance."

Sensible lady.

Her children were a boy and a girl. And you can't have an older boy and a girl share one room. So I had to work with what was at hand. A house with two bedrooms. One for the kids. One for the parents. Since holidays and summers happen predictably, both children would be home at the same time, or surely overlap part of the time.

Mrs. Fine had already moved in and done most of the house herself, so she'd only need me as a consulting decorator, which costs less money.

First, we'd look at the second bedroom. Was it big enough to divide? One indication that it might be would be two windows, each on a different wall, spaced far apart. Even in a small room, this means you can separate the sleeping areas by some form of divider.

But the bedroom she had planned to use for the kids had one window wall in a fairly narrow room. So making it into two rooms was an impossibility. (You *can* divide a wide window wall with a slim partition.)

Before we gave up on the splitting of the kids' future room, I suggested we look at the bedroom she and Mr. Fine had only recently moved into. It provided the solution. The master bedroom was a bigger room and had two separated windows. They'd switch rooms.

Think simple when it comes to dividing one room. Forget complicated room dividers, those endless-component structures that supposedly give storage space while acting as walls. They take up too much floor space, anyway.

We had to devise a way to make one room into *two* closed-off separate sleeping cubicles for use at night. With a small entry hall *within* the room itself. We'd be making two private rooms with two private entrances inside one room.

The easiest way to do the job was to use accordion-fold ceiling-hung dividers of heavy plasticized fabric. (You've seen them used as temporary partitions in doctors' offices, in hotel-motel meeting rooms.)

Two separate sets would be needed. Looking at the ceiling in the room you want to divide will give you the clue: you'll see that you'll need a T-shaped pattern of drapery hardware tracks on the ceiling. Hung so that each sleep area will have its own extra wall and entrance door. (They even have locks for privacy hounds.) Hung correctly, they open with ease, and afford, unlike *any* permanent structure, a spacious look in the daytime. They come in attractive textures and wide color ranges, so don't worry about their institutional derivation. Order them in the same light-color category as the walls and floors for bigger space feeling.

Place the beds in position before you install *anything.* Use single beds as far apart as possible, each near its own window. Then have a professional installer put in your folding walls.

The sleep section nearest the room entrance should be for the most consistent night owl.

Each bed should have its own chest–night table with as much drawer space as possible. Use wall-hung spotlighting fixtures that swivel, for reading and bed lighting. (They take up no surface space on bedside furniture.)

The single beds can have completely different, unmatching bed coverings. Don't use big bolster cushions. You can always have small throw cushions or slipcovered bed pillows to get a couch effect. They're used either at night, if they're the bed pillows, or can be thrown under the bed if they're throw cushions. Big bolsters take up too much floor space when not in use. If we chose, say, a green, yellow, and white plaid cover for the male bed, we could use a solid pale yellow quilted one for the female bed.

And each private window can be done individually, too—perhaps to match the bedcovers.

The His and Hers solid walls—the *actual* room walls—must remain private property. For favorite photographs, posters, or wall-hung shelving.

If there's one closet in the room, it could be one big problem. If possible, I'd like to see it used for shelf-storage space. The top for him, the bottom for her. But if *her* bed winds up near the closet, then the closet should be hers. Girls require more privacy in dressing than boys. If necessary, give over an outer hall closet to the pair and divide it into two separate sections for hanging their clothing.

Meanwhile, consider floor-standing individual coat-and-hat racks. There are slim bentwood ones that look terrific, almost like sculpture. They'll hold a day's supply of clothes and a robe for trips to bathrooms, etc. Buy two.

If there's enough space in the newly created inner hall, a narrow wall-hung shelf could serve as a dual desk. With two slender chairs for the desk—or other use. Here's where a wall mirror would serve well, and their mutual telephone could be on the shelf desk, too. And the one small attractive table lamp that works from the wall switch. *No* ceiling lighting in a room with ceiling-hung dividers.

We divided and conquered. Mrs. Fine liked the newly furnished rooms within a room. So did Mr. Fine.

But how about the collegians in their nighttime cubicles? Had I made two claustrophobic enemies? Well, the girl called me on their first trip home.

"Mrs. Clark, when I'm in my bed at night, I feel as if I'm inside an envelope, but it's a thank-you-note envelope. It says, 'Thank you for being home.' My brother? Well, he's in love at the moment, so he's not around much, but he likes the idea of being able to lock a *wall* shut so he can lie on his bed and stare at the ceiling. You know what? He's got his girl's picture glued on the ceiling over his bed! Isn't that the *dumbest thing* you ever heard?"

I thought it was fine.

MOURNER NUMBER FIVE:

The dumbest thing I ever heard is the story of Mourner Number Five. Namely, me.

You will remember that I was solving the problem of what to do about my own son's room by keeping his door shut. Jeff's door stayed shut for an incredibly long time after he left, while I roamed around the apartment, all upset and feeling sorry for myself. Maybe because Jeff and I had been living alone together. He in the big bedroom and I in the smaller one. Mine was splendidly decorated, of course. But not his. He didn't want any decorator ideas in his room. All he wanted in his was retail furniture he'd chosen himself.

Professionals have trouble dealing with personal problems in their own fields. Doctors rarely ask to operate on their wives; shoemakers, according to legend, never make shoes for themselves or their families. They can't seem to keep a steady hand or level head about those near and dear to them.

Dinny, who had gone through the very same rigors with *my* aid and survived the departure of her daughter, responded to my plight by suggesting that I keep his room exactly the way it was. "Just add a photograph of Jeff in cap and gown," she said. "And burn candles in front of it. Like a shrine."

It took the aid, as well as the insults, of many friends, relatives, and clients to get me moving.

The Newly Childless Household

I looked around the room. It needed a heavy cleaning.

Okay, so at least I had something to start me off. The hiring of outside help for heavy cleaning. The extra cleaning help cost money. But a nice room appeared. What space, what possibilities—however, I could hear Jeff's voice ringing in my ears: "I don't want any decorator in my room."

So I wrote him a letter. I didn't request a reply, because I was firmly convinced that he was so busy writing the great American novel that he had no time to write me. I wrote a short note saying that I'd received an offer of twenty-three dollars for the entire contents of his room. And that I would redecorate it for him, after the sale, at no cost whatever to him.

The phone rang two days later, and on the other end of the line was the sound of Jeff's voice. (After the sound of the operator's voice asking the usual collect-phone-call questions.)

As much as I am onto Jeff, he is onto me. "You wouldn't sell that stuff for any twenty-three dollars, Mom. What's the matter?"

"Just wondering if you'd like your room redone while you're away."

"Well, why not?"

"But, Jeff, you always told me you didn't want me in there doing anything, so I didn't know. . . ."

"That's when I was *there*. But now I'm in college, I don't want to come back to any high school room. Gee, I thought you'd have it all done by now."

"Well, not quite. I was wondering, for instance, what your favorite colors might be."

"Come on, Mom. You never ask a client that. You've told me they never know for sure. All they're ever sure of is the color they hate. Okay, I hate pink."

"Okay."

The Not So Terrible Move

End of phone call. Beginning of a fresh lease on life for me. I was now free to go into his room and do it as if he were my client.

There were a few problems, even with the new approach. Because the new client's room happened to be in my apartment, and his decorator happened to be his mother.

The major cleaning job done, there were several cartons of old clothing waiting to be picked up by the Salvation Army. Those kindly folk not only pick up almost anything that's fairly usable but a contribution is tax deductible.

Rich from having received a tax deduction, I proceeded to have his room wallpapered. I chose a good scrubbable white paper. It was applied to three walls, two of which had shelving on them. All the shelving had to be removed in order for the paperhanger to do the job. Then all the shelving had to be reinstalled. I looked at the three newly done walls with all the shelving and their attendant books back in place. *Then* I realized: Who needs scrubbable wallpaper in back of books?

One mistake noted, I proceeded.

The remaining wall, which had always held his pictures and the usual posters, was awaiting a very special paper. A rich-looking straw cloth. It was not only rich-looking, it was priced for people who *are*. When the paperhanger came back to put it on, he noted that it needed a lining; so his price went up beyond his original estimate. But the paper was beautiful.

Another mistake duly recorded: I would never have let that happen to a regular client.

The door to Jeff's room was constantly open because the workmen I had hired and I were working in it. It was then that I decided to move our one TV set into his room. That would give me a reason to use the room while he was away. This meant calling in the cable-TV men. We had been hooked into cable TV almost the minute it became available, because it not only gave us access to many extra channels but also because our reception had given us a picture that resembled oatmeal.

A little extra work came up when the cable guys had to drill through walls and closets to install the new cable extension. As they drilled through the small closet in Jeff's room, I saw something amazing. The closet held only two tennis rackets. All his stored-away horde took up only half of the big double closet in his hallway. So I moved my long dresses and coats into his empty small closet. He had plenty of space and, finally, I could have uncrushed dress-up clothing.

As I tried to relax on his bed one evening during the renovation, to see a well-executed murder on television, I realized that the bed had not been replaced since he was about twelve. Good heavens! Everybody gets a new bed. Nearly all my clients do. This one could be no exception.

I ordered a bed for him. I had received many ads and brochures extolling the virtues of this particular bed: made entirely of wooden slats that would flex with the contours of the body, it was covered by a simple slender mattress of special foam. It sounded fascinating, it was expensive, and it would take less room than his old bed. I must add that I ordered it by phone and that it came quickly.

After admiring its covering, I lay down on it and discovered something about myself. I was a loaf of bread being gently sliced. I could feel the flexible blades coming to get me through the trim, thin mattress. Fortunately, Jeff has more upholstery on his bones than I do, so I hoped maybe he wouldn't feel it so much, though I realized quickly that I'd made a mistake. Never order a bed without having tested it, or without knowing a great deal about it and its manufacturer. (I ordered a new mattress for it fast, of course.)

The Not So Terrible Move

Jeff came home for Christmas and was delighted. He congratulated me. And proceeded to ask friends in to see the room and to attend parties.

I was contented with other festivities, such as cooking, cleaning, and answering phone calls—all of which were for him. He couldn't hear his phone ringing, because he had taken to wearing earphones so that he could listen to records while watching ice hockey.

Of course, when I was invited out to a Christmas or New Year's party, I had trouble getting dressed because my fancy clothes were in his room in my newly acquired closet. The trouble was I needed a pilot's license to navigate my way through his room. It had become an electronic showroom. Covering most of the décor.

Using his room as the complete family den was out. I bought myself a portable TV set, put it in my room, and waited for him to leave.

He left.

He returned.

This sequence continued. Each time he left, I'd go into his room and rearrange it enough so that perhaps some of the wallpaper might show or the bed might be used for an overnight guest.

Just as I got accustomed to the idea that the room would remain Jeff's no matter whether he was home or not, he returned on another vacation bringing with him his new roommate. A dog. He announced that he was going to live in an apartment off campus, packed up most of his furnishings, electrical gear, a lot of the better accessories, and moved. Aside from leaving the draperies, the bed, and the carpeting, he left the dog. I like that dog almost as much as he does. And I'm stuck with it twice as much.

Now I do whatever I wish with Jeff's room while he's away,

knowing he'll do something else with it every time he comes back.

All us former mourners are in agreement. The room of the departing child must become the room ready for the returning young adult. In decorating terminology, I think you might call it "ultra-flexible spontaneous."

～9～

The Stuck-in-the-House Wife

"Duvie, I've never used a decorator, because I wanted my house to be me. Well, it's me, all right . . . miserable."

I was sitting in the small den of a house in the suburbs listening to an attractive young woman. Her story was one I'd heard before, but with variations. Houses and their owners are like fingerprints: the differences may be slight but very telling.

The difference that became apparent first was that no one who wasn't told would ever know that the lady, *or* her house, was miserable.

Her name was Thea. She was good-looking, young, married, with three children, a newish house, a car, a cat, a dog; and she had friends who raved about her. In fact, I had met her through one of those friends, whose house I'd done.

But decorators have to learn the inside story. If there weren't some sort of problem, I wouldn't have been there.

Thea sat curled up on an old worn couch; I sat opposite her on a chair that could have been described the same way. As I glanced to my right, I could see her living room. Looked nice and bright. Living rooms usually are the best rooms in a house —why weren't we sitting in there rather than in this cramped room with its obviously haphazard furnishings?

The Stuck-in-the-House Wife

One answer occurred to me immediately. She was saving the living room for Sundays. Sounds odd, I know, but it's a fairly popular phenomenon that has spread like the flu. The virus that is its source is the little or big room known as the DEN. This extra room, this supposed boon, is striven for and achieved by means both fair and freak. I have seen families move from cooped-up apartments or minuscule houses, only to take over a small part of their new basement and turn it into a den. In it goes all the old furniture.

I have seen families buy houses from plans *only* because the new house has a den. For all the old furniture.

In this extra room also goes one other group of old things: the whole family. Because this is the safe room. Everything in it is already worn, so nothing can be damaged. Nothing, that is, except the pride and the comfort that a planned move should offer.

Having a den has nothing to do with having money. You'll find them in huge dream houses with lots of acreage and small subdivision homes with lawns big enough only for a hedge clipper; even apartments suddenly serve up a tiny extra room. The culprit-den has led to the kind of house I call "immobilized." The house becomes under-utilized, its householders hibernating in a cavelike room, while the rest of the house sits around almost unused.

If your den has you trapped, you will soon feel it. The symptoms are:

A slight sensation of imprisonment.
An overly clean living room.
A feeling that your house isn't giving you your money's worth.

"You know?" said Thea. "Sometimes I don't know why we even bothered to move. . . . Somehow we don't seem to be any

201

more comfortable than we were in our smaller place. Oh, I don't know—this whole thing is too much for me."

The fact was, of course, the house was not *enough* for her. She had den disease, all right.

But that wasn't all. She had another very popular ailment. Commonly known as "fear of decorators." She revealed it to me in an admirably straightforward manner.

"Frankly, Duvie," she continued, "if I hadn't seen that house you decorated near here—if I hadn't met you and asked about you—I would never have called a decorator. I think I'm afraid of them."

It's not unusual to be afraid of decorators, or lawyers, or dentists—or anyone you call because you're in sudden need. Or pain.

"All I can say, Thea, is *I* don't like houses that look decorated. An obviously decorated house is as bad as an overdressed woman. *And* just as uncomfortable."

Decorating is supposedly one of the arts. But, I think, properly done, it is one of the humanities. It is no admission of failure to say you need a decorator. You can't treat a troubled house with an aspirin any more than you'd paint over a skin rash. Recognizing that a problem exists is one of the steps on the way to curing it. Thea had been too embarrassed to admit she'd failed at making her house come out right, and her usual competency had almost locked her in a place she didn't even like.

"Does it always cost a fortune to decorate?" she asked.

"It can. But it doesn't have to. The right decorator works with her client so that they control the expenditures wisely. Getting the right decorator can be a task. The best way to do it is to look around a lot, and ask a lot of questions. Just like you've been doing, Thea."

The Stuck-in-the-House Wife

"But," she asked, "how can you say to a friend whose house you like, 'How much did it cost?'"

"You probably can't. Not right out. But you can ask, 'Are you happy with the job? Did it work out pretty much the way you wanted it to?' And you'll get an odd assortment of answers."

1. *"Oh, we just love the way the house looks."* (With that answer, check for further details. The answer should have said a little something about the way the house works.)

2. *"Someday we'll get through paying for it—but isn't it just gorgeous?"* (They should be telling you it's gorgeous and not asking you. And, re paying for it, these particular pals may *want* you to think it cost more than it did. Or *they* may only be happy with expensive. You have to know *them* pretty well.)

3. *"We're happy here. And we certainly got what we wanted. Our decorator watched the prices with us. Some things were expensive, others weren't. In the end, we came out just fine, and I think you should use our decorator—if you ever need one."* That's the kind of answer you're waiting for. And that's the kind of friend you should hope for: one who suggests help only if *you* want it. She's not saying, "You sure *need* a decorator. You've *got* to use our decorator!" Best of all, she's stated the truth about cost: "In the end, we came out just fine."

Of course, there's always the business of "the most popular decorator in town," whose work is seen all around town. Having developed a passion for pink, this interior designer is painting the town pink. (Since I have been through a green stage myself, I can only commiserate.) What happens is that everyone's house begins to look alike. Friends become enemies. And then the worst enemy of them all becomes the interior designer. Who is at fault? Everyone.

The Not So Terrible Move

Some women look great in miniskirts. But maybe you don't. So you have sense enough not to wear them. When hems sag to the ankles, possibly you hold to the line you like. You keep your head and show your legs. So keep your head about your house. Your house is not a passing fancy and it's not as easy to fix as a hemline.

A decorator must be flexible according to his or her client, and the client must use logic when dealing with a decorator. Several tardy deliveries, disappearing workmen, a few taste conflicts—these are almost reason enough to give up and try again with someone else. But what if the client becomes worried about the endless bills and their size? Let us say that an unusually high bill came in from your decorator. Let us say that, after the first shock, you rechecked and discovered a mistake in simple arithmetic. Instead of hitting the ceiling, dial the phone. Tell your decorator about the mistake. Working well together, you can avoid most of the problems. If some prices really are too high, ask about them, too. You'll get an informed answer, and you may decide together to switch to another price line or postpone some projects. The art of communicating is an important one for decorators and their clients.

Thea had listened attentively as I explained this. She seemed comforted, but still confused. She felt that her house had not only gotten away from her but she had thought too much about the problems involved in fixing it, so now she had enough extra problems for an entire community.

It was time for a fast, tangible treatment. I arranged to get invited to stay for dinner. I had to get to know Thea's family and how they had grown to misusing this house.

When the children got home from school, each headed for the kitchen for food first aid. They then left opened empty boxes and bottles behind them, and each went to a room.

From every child's room came sound. A telephone rang. Records or radios were playing loudly. A cat which had been asleep on the den couch was now scratching at a child's door. A dog which had been curled up on my feet while we'd been talking in the den was now racing up and down a hall trying to outrun a Frisbee and outhowl a multiphonic sound system.

Thea yelled at someone to get the phone. It was for her. It was her husband, Lew; he'd be late. He had a conference with a special customer.

Thea was getting upset with everyone and everything. She said, "It seems as if I'm always stuck waiting for Lew. Or dashing to the station to pick him up while we're in the middle of eating dinner, because he's just a *little* late. Or very late."

Lew, whom I'd met at a party, was at the stage in his life where he was busy getting ahead. I remember his saying, when he was told I was a decorator, "Tell me, doesn't anyone ever design a house where a man can cry sanctuary?"

Sanctuary. A protected hideaway. Or, according to him, a place of his own—inside his own home—where he could be alone when he needed to be.

Thea started dashing and darting to get the dining-room table set. She stopped when one child asked, "Company coming?"

In other words, they didn't usually use the dining room.

She looked at me questioningly, "Do you mind?"

"I'm not company. . . . I'm your decorator."

And we prepared to eat, as they usually did, in the kitchen.

Now more sound came—from the den this time. A fight about which child was to see what television show.

Finally we sat down to eat, with everyone but Lew assembled at the round dinette table in the kitchen. It was foodproof and childproof, but there wasn't enough room on it for the platters of good food Thea had prepared, and she was constantly getting up to add more things.

Then the phone rang. It was Lew—at the station. So Thea rushed for the car to pick him up. I stayed with the children, who bolted most of the rest of their food, left most of the dishes, and jammed others into the already full dishwasher.

One boy went back into the den and turned on television. The others went to their rooms. But the sounds did not abate.

When Thea and Lew returned, she busied herself clearing a place at the table for him and reheating food. He went into the den to leave his briefcase. I heard a brief conversation between father and son.

"When I've eaten, I want you *out* of here. You see the work I've got to do? And what's that mess on my desk? Can't you use your *own* desk for your papers?"

"But we're s'posed to watch this show for school. And I'm gonna take notes. . . ."

An angered father came to dinner, finally.

Both Thea and Lew, the couple in the immobilized home, were controlling themselves because I was with them. But they seemed ready for a fight.

He had come home hoping for the quiet he knew he wouldn't find. She stayed home, waiting for him, waiting on the children, waiting for something to happen that would assuage the angry hurt she was always covering.

The house was in rebellion.

I suggested we take our coffee into the living room where the three of us could talk quietly. They glanced at each other. Evidently they did not often take coffee in the living room. Well, it's a small form of elegance. And elegance is a form of planned peace. They certainly needed a little peace.

We had to pull up chairs to talk comfortably. The room was arranged with cornered seating. If you're constantly pulling chairs around in order to have a living room to talk in, then you can be sure the living room is wrong.

The Stuck-in-the-House Wife

Lew put his feet up. On the cocktail table next to the coffee cups. On the couch, Thea uncomfortably fumbled with a cup and saucer, looking as if she'd like to stretch out. But she didn't. She was probably saving the couch cover.

"Thea's always envying other people's houses." Lew said this to me. He was in a chair so small he looked like an hors d'oeuvre impaled on four toothpicks.

"Most people do. It's not odd, really. You're luckier than most. . . . Your house can be made enviable."

It was important right then for Lew to think about his home as a place for others to admire. Because his career was in its growing stage, he needed a place to bring his customers. To entertain friends. To show off. (And I mean that very positively. A man who is house-proud can also be wife-proud, family-proud. It's a kind of pride that's not false.)

First I had to get them to use the living room.

There is a relatively easy way to do it. Since they had always lived in their den, eaten in their kitchen, we had to make the living room casual. And the fastest way to do it? Rearrange the furniture already in the room. Don't even think about new pieces until you've juggled around what you already own.

We finished coffee and, with the aid of the oldest boy, started pushing furniture.

No matter what—move your present couch. It's usually the biggest piece of furnishing in the room and the most permanently planted. Release it from its accustomed spot and you're immediately challenged.

We let it stick out into the room. It became a natural divider. The empty couch wall could now take a large wooden piece of furniture. We moved a long chest that held a record player. Strangely enough, the picture arrangement that had been over the couch looked right and less rigidly planned over the big chest.

The Not So Terrible Move

One large lamp placed on the chest lit the whole wall. The accustomed pair of lamps from each side of the couch were then able to split, amicably, to be used somewhere else.

The two delicate chairs (one of which had semi-supported Lew) looked fine silhouetted at each side of the chest. That one wall—the long important living-room wall—became informal but attractive. A good place for music to come from, for pictures to be looked at.

"Lew," I asked, "the desk in the den—can we try it in here? It's quieter in here at night. It might be a good place for you to work. Especially when the kids are watching TV in the den." It made sense to him.

A man's desk in the living room makes a section of the room not only handsome but useful.

We placed the desk in a far corner, in front of a built-in bookcase. The bookcase's bottom shelves could hold Lew's work papers, books, briefcase; they would not only be available, but unseen, because the large desk, placed far enough away to allow for a desk chair, would hide the bookcase bottom from sight.

His desk chair was brought in from the den. We tried it behind the desk so that it faced into the room. He liked it that way. But none of us liked the old desk lamp, so we used one of the matched pair formerly at couch side. A bright, tall brass lamp. Distinctive.

A desk must look important in its new living-room role. The good lamp helped. Perhaps the desk would need refinishing, and a desk set would be a fine idea. A handsome inkwell—a massive paperweight. Surely a big attractive wastebasket would enhance the work area. Lew was becoming more and more interested in the decorating project. No one had to tell him; he saw it happen. He'd have his own special sanctuary.

"How about an easy chair and an ottoman in front of the

desk . . . facing the couch?" (We'd pushed the couch farther off-center; it was closer to the windows, and there was more open floor space for seating.)

Lew's old easy chair that was so comfortable in the den looked awful in the living room. Because it was comfortable and beloved, it needed thought. Actually, it was like an old family cow—good in the right place. Never in the living room. Inspecting it, I discovered that it needed rebuilding, then re-covering or slipcovering. The added cost of having an ottoman made to go with it—well, the whole deal would have cost as much and made as much sense as redesigning a cow. Now they started thinking about buying a new chair, but it was only *after* we had seen and tried what they already owned.

We hauled in more chairs from other rooms. Just to plan our seating. When that was done, we could see what tables would be necessary, what lighting would be needed. Good furnishings should be able to be moved from room to room without looking out of place. This is especially true of chairs, lamps, pictures; sometimes even a chest of drawers; surely a desk. The room was being arranged in a circle. The corners were being used, but the actual seating plan itself was circular, which I've always called tribal, following the ancient instinct to sit close together, warmly. Sitting around. Literally.

Their cocktail table was long, rectangular, a knee-bruiser and, of course, a couch-blocker. We might use it in another room, but for this couch and the chairs that would circle around it, we'd need a round table. One that would have a slightly higher central pedestal, so no legs. Its height would make it reachable without stooping; the circular shape would mean you could move around it without getting hurt. More than two people could then sit on the couch, and there would be no odd man out in the middle, because the whole couch would be approachable.

One of the old end tables that had "book-ended" the couch

now sat on the window side of the newly placed couch and held the other brass lamp, whose mate was on the desk. So now the pair of lamps were on opposite sides of the room. Each at the same level, but far apart. A pair of lamps placed far apart—at the same height—give a spacious feeling. Yet they are not static, repetitive, boring.

Opposite the desk corner was another set of matching built-in bookcases. All at the far end of the room. Here the room could use a portable TV set for adult viewing. With a simple mobile stand, it would "disappear" against the active bookcase display and yet be viewable from any spot in the room. Any easy chairs we'd buy would have casters, so they would move easily to make for informal comfort, but they wouldn't need to be shoved around for group seating. (Casters on chairs are nice to have even if you don't use them often. If you don't have them when they are needed, they are like the tissues you forgot to put in your purse.)

It was important to give this newly planned comfortable living room the enviable glamor Thea and Lew wanted—to make it the impressive room they both really needed.

They had to have a beautiful permanent slipcover on the couch, splendidly cut, so that its cushions would be truly reversible, and easily removable for cleaning. Some permanent slipcovers are actually tacked into place around the bottom so that there is no saggy look. (If there's a skirt on the couch, tacking is not needed.) The slipcover fabric would be a heavy woven one imprinted with much pattern, looking like linen, but without linen's tendency to wrinkle. The all-over pattern wouldn't show dirt. We'd choose something exotic. It would cost money, but it would look impressive, be long-lasting, and be one less thing for Thea to worry about.

The same fabric could be used at the windows. But we didn't

really need full draw-draperies because their window wall faced a view. A view itself can be redone. Decorate outdoors so that there's something good to look out at. A rock garden, softly spotlit at night, is beautiful even in winter. If you face a street at the edge of your lawn, plant high evergreen trees in a clump.

We'd use wall-hung draperies on each side of the window and a simply shaped cornice across the top, covered to match.

But, as we all know, no window should always be unshielded. (A party can be seen from the outside, by the one person you forgot to invite.) Vertical blinds are worth investigating. They look like straight, up-and-down ribbons. They glide open and shut like standard draperies, yet, when shut, they can angle for closed-off privacy or become slim panels letting in the light.

Their easy chairs? An easy chair can be any size, shape, or style. As long as it's comfortable, it's easy. Lew's chair should certainly be bought with *his* shape in mind. But the three others we decided to buy could be low, curved, tufted—done in nylon velvet or suède, or leather, or fake leather. Whatever the fabric, if they were not skirted to the floor they'd seem to "float." Anytime you can see the floor under a piece of furniture, your room will look bigger.

The objects on the coffee table, on the top shelves of the bookcases, on the surface of the long music chest would be "collectors' items." And that doesn't have to mean a lot of money. It simply means a collection you have assembled. Copperware, brass, porcelains can be collected inexpensively if you use care and stick to one type of item. If you're willing to start with some chipped or slightly damaged pieces, you'll pay a lot less—and an antique dealer is delighted to see a beginning collector. (He knows you'll become an addict.) Reproductions of early brasses or copper can start you off. Then you'll find out that the genuine thing will cost you less in the long run. Your eye will learn to spot quality and age under a layer of tarnish. We'd put new frames on old pictures and new pictures in old-looking handsome frames.

The lamp bases would be worth lighting. Lampshades would be brand-new. A beautiful lamp can make a mediocre piece of furniture look like a fine one.

Forget about the "focal point." That's the ancient adage that says each room should have one glorious spot to focus your eyes on. Nuts. Wherever you sit or stand, you should have something lovely to look at.

A well-decorated room fascinates slowly. The first effect is one of welcome and comfort. Then objects beckon—pictures attract, plants loom softly—the room enfolds its guests. Perhaps questions about the collection are asked, so conversations change, moods change. A living room should be alive.

But their dining room, like many others, was deadly. They were afraid of it. It was dark, the table scratched easily, the two silver candlesticks on it stood like guards in a barracks protecting the stale-looking centerpiece. The buffet was in the same dark, easily scratched wood. It was a cold, uninviting dining room. It intimidated the very people who should have enjoyed it.

They feared that the rug and the chair seats would get stained, the tabletop would be ruined—all the popular worries in the unused dining room. And all unnecessary.

To get a dining room into use fast, buy a serving cart with big easy-roll wheels—and enough shelf space. You can serve from it, clear off with it. It's a magnificent servant on wheels.

To forget worrying about the rug, go look at vinyl flooring. But don't, unintentionally, spend as much on vinyl as on marble. Don't choose a tile that requires many separate pieces to be put together by workmen who do fine work, slowly, and who get paid by the hour. Oddly enough, a small room looks larger with a large tile pattern on the floor. (Don't forget the classically elegant black-and-white checkerboard. I've never seen it fail to add glamour and brilliance to a room.) If you're anti-tile and pro-wood, you can have your wooden floor scraped, stained, and polished. But remember, the higher the luster, the more possibility you have of slipping. If you *must* have a dining-room rug, be sure it's big enough to allow you and your guests to push back the chairs without falling off the edge of the rug. It's a sensation I've experienced and it's shattering. (Also shattered the cup and saucer I was holding.)

Wallpaper goes well in dining rooms. If you want light and brilliance in the room, don't buy a tiny overall pattern. Think of something you can "see through," such as a white background with a large latticework pattern or widely spaced vines on a light background. The idea is to feel as though you're in a garden, on a picnic.

As for that intimidating table, the top can be refinished with a coating that will render it impervious to almost anything. A good furniture refinisher will know what to recommend. Beware of the really heavy plastic coatings. I've seen some that make tabletops look like tabletop-in-aspic. If you don't add extra leaves to the table often, you can have a glass top cut for it. Whatever solution you choose, have the buffet top redone the same way. Or add a much patterned marble top to the buffet, so you can put a hot platter on it.

Think of your dining room as a natural extension of your kitchen, which happens to be what it is.

The dining-room chair seats can be a solid-color leather-looking vinyl. Or a spray-protected fabric. Or cane, with removable seat cushions.

Have a pretty chandelier. You can have a rheostat installed on your light switch so that you can dim it or brighten it. Bright for dining, dim for clearing.

The Not So Terrible Move

Open your dining-room windows. At least let them make you *feel* as if they were open, with pulled-to-the-sides drapery fabric that matches your wallpaper, and plants at the windows, catching light. Venetian blinds will let you control the problems of light and view. Inveterate haters of standard Venetian blinds have changed their point of view: there are blinds with skinny metal slats and hardly visible strings, no fabric tapes at all—they almost disappear from sight when they're open. Closed, their color can be sky or sun. So the dining-room windows can seem always magically open.

Use informal objects to decorate your table. Forget stuffy-looking centerpieces. Put a mass of small potted plants on a tray, all in a low, big basket you can remove from the table quickly. Get bright, large salt-and-pepper shakers—two sets—one for each end of the table. Use your buffet for things you need to serve with: sugar bowl and creamer, breadbasket. Silver candle-sticks? Have them cleaned and lacquered professionally; then put them together at one end of the buffet—ready for use, but casually shown.

If your dining room opens off the living room and can be seen from it, *remove the doors.* Remember it will be lovely to look at, the lighting can be dimmed when your table is being cleared, and your serving cart will have done the work quickly.

A house is a mass of rooms—with doors. Doors can mean instant privacy or complete inconvenience. A view of an attractive dining room can be hindered by doors. But the kitchen door leading to the dining room should be thought about carefully. If you always have it open, remove it. If you use it to hinder cooking odors from spreading, then be sure the door is hinged so that it stays open or shut without hitting you in the face as you go through it.

If a noisy den has no doors, *add* them. They can be hinged

The Stuck-in-the-House Wife

like screens so that they open gracefully and are right architecturally.

Doors well placed can make rooms work better, because they not only add efficiency but they also subtract noise.

The talk about silence led Thea, Lew, and me back into the hall containing all the bedrooms. The hall was a miniature speedway, its bare floor constantly reverberating to the sounds of kids and animals racing. Here's where indoor-outdoor carpeting would come in. The traction is good, but not good enough for roller skates. And any falls would be cushioned.

Their children's rooms, as so often happens, seemed to consist of furnishings made of plastic, enameled wood, or metal. Their floors were made of washable linoleum. Any fabrics were thin. They seemed to be rooms designed to be cleaned by a powerful fire hose. All this marvelously childproof stuff is a great sound conductor. Sound bounces off and echoes through rooms with all that hard surfacing.

For children's rooms one should:

Use heavy curtaining fabric.
Get heavyweight bedspreads.
Buy large slip-proof throw rugs.
Cork at least one wall.
Use felt wallpaper wherever possible.
Add an extra panel to the bedroom door for insulation.

For the musically inclined offspring, install an acoustic-tile ceiling. As long as you're at it, think of each child as a future musical prodigy and get enough acoustic tiling to do all their ceilings.

All these additions can be colorful, stylish, and low on maintenance. Also low in price. Your children will be delighted with

215

their specially created living quarters. And you'll live longer and more peacefully.

It is said that a third of our lives is spent between sheets—in a bedroom. So after Thea, Lew, and I had wandered from the children's rooms down to the end of the hall to their bedroom, I hoped they were insomniacs by choice. *That* room was no place to sleep in. Or live in. Or relax in.

They had planned to wait to redo their room.

You can't wait to rest. You can't wait away a third of your life.

Their bedroom was filled with odd furnishings. A queen-size bed (a bed that's somewhat larger than a double bed, and a lot smaller than a king-size bed) had a headboard that supported strange clip-on lamps and featured much chipped paint. It had obviously done a lot of moving and not benefited from the exercise.

The mattress was low on one side, high on the other. They'd waited too long to remember to turn it; now it would have to be replaced. On either side of the tired bed were two bedside chests. Originally unpainted wood, they were still unpainted, so that stains from coffee cups and water glasses showed distinctly. Several round wooden pulls were missing from the drawers.

A tall dark chest of drawers was placed next to a long low chest of drawers—all directly opposite the bed. There seemed to be a plateau and then a mountain of mismatched wood. A huge lamp covered most of the large mirror that had been hung over the low chest.

There was a desklike structure that housed a sewing machine jammed into a corner, without enough room for real sewing comfort. Its chair was covered with clothes, robes—the usual bedroom things that wind up on chairs till they're put away. Another chair must have been from Thea's girlhood home. Faded, lumpy, it could barely support the extra quilt that had landed on it.

There were heavy draperies, many pictures hung at weird levels, magazines and books piled into a magazine rack that listed from loss of one leg. And a folded card table in full view.

"You play cards in here?" I asked Thea, who was looking embarrassed.

"No, sometimes I open it to fold clothes on or to use for sewing supplies. I need someplace to come and work quietly. I have a wide choice of escaping to the kitchen or an empty bathroom."

Lew looked at Thea and said, "I think maybe the bedroom should be done now, too."

The first thing I needed to know was what all that drawer space was used for. Either they had more clothes, or more unused clothing, than most couples or, more likely, they had just kept what they had and given no thought to excess furniture *or* clothing.

My first suggestion was that they check to see if they *needed* all that drawer space. Next was a question about Lew's shirts. Since many men wear drip-dry shirts, the addition of an extra pole in his closet could mean storage area without the purchase of an expensive piece of furniture. Why buy anything you don't really need? Well-thought-out closets can save lots of money on bedroom chests.

One chest at bedside might serve for Lew's things and give him plenty of surface for a presentable reading lamp and books and magazines. A tall, very narrow chest, called a "semainier," can be the answer for women's lingerie. (A semainier features seven drawers. The French way of saying one drawer for each day of the week. Anyway, they're graceful—and nigh onto perfect for those sets of panties embroidered with "Monday," "Tuesday," "Wednesday," etc.)

At Thea's bedside, she could use another small chest, or a table, or even a drop-leaf desk opened to hold her lamp, book,

217

and coffee cup. A lovely small chair there would serve many purposes, too.

Since it was obvious that the bedroom would be Thea's personal sanctuary, I had to give her something special in it. That something special would be the luxury of a chaise longue. After much questioning, I've discovered that women do not like to lie down on a made-up bed. A chaise longue combines privacy, glamour, rest, and is exotically sensible. Before you dream up white satin like a Mae West movie (which isn't exactly horrible but is a trifle impractical), think of being able to stretch out with your feet up, during the day, fully dressed, without worrying about the furniture. There's your place to read, to talk on the phone; the phone company can put the bedroom phone on a "jack" near the chaise.

You can purchase a standard chaise longue in a better department store. It's usually in a tufted chintz or velvet. Also, it's usually expensive. If you can't find what you like and can afford in the chaise longue section, try the wrought-iron porch-furniture department. They'll have wicker pieces there, too. An outside-type chaise, its cushioning slipcovered to match your bed cover—painted a bedroom color—becomes the most comfortable piece of furniture in the world. Use feminine soft little cushions on it, a throw blanket at its foot. Placed near a window, next to a table, it takes up very little space and does a very big job.

Since Thea and Lew both agreed that the bedroom would be her special place, there wasn't the usual problem of combining masculine and feminine in décor. It would be a feminine bedroom. They mutually agreed on mossy green with coral. I'd search out fabrics and rugs while they got rid of unnecessary things and bulky pieces.

One piece that would leave their bedroom immediately was Thea's sewing machine. We hauled it into the den. There Thea would have plenty of space to sew during the day when the kids were away. With Lew's den desk now in the living room, the sewing-machine desk had space. Painted a bright color, it would be a nice place for an overnight guest to have a morning cup of coffee or to write a note. The overnight guest would be supplied with a sleep sofa. (We'd slipcover the big old couch in a handsome but inexpensive fabric that was sturdy enough for feet and paws but not too rough for elbows.) The little sleep sofa would replace the big old worn-out easy chair. So the den would become a guest room, a sewing room, a kids' TV-viewing room; in other words, it would become the extra-dividend room it should be. An adjunct to the living room when its soon-to-be-installed doors were opened. Or a private haven with its doors shut

We walked through to the kitchen and realized that it was really in need of nothing except a place for Thea to sit while working at a counter too high for a chair. And desperately in need of garbage cans for those natural litterers, the children.

We could fill the two needs with the addition of a well-designed garbage container. A tall slender metal can with a wooden top—cut to fit and upholstered, like a seat, in plastic—would give extra seating and plenty of container space for constant debris. (Actually, with garbage-container bags, or lightweight inner containers, anything from a nail keg to an oil drum can be used as a trash container. If you can utilize the top for seating, your kitchen will not only be a lot cleaner but more comfortable, as well.)

It could be difficult to change the habit patterns of this family. Always eating in the kitchen might take time to outgrow. But the rolling serving cart would make kitchen dining easier, too. And if Thea was more rested because she had a place of her own to rest in, using the dining room at dinnertime would be more of a delight than a chore.

The Not So Terrible Move

Relaxation can spread around a house. Like consideration, it can be catching.

Thea would have to continue playing the waiting game while her home was being redone, but she would be building a house rather than tearing herself apart.

The immobilized home—the stuck-in-the-house wife? They slowly, slowly changed.

Their guests were, I hope, enchanted with the pleasant re-done entry hall. With its closet because it had empty hangers ready for coats, with its beautiful chandelier that lit a turquoise ceiling, and with its clean, clear elegance. (Too small really to furnish—we used a three-tier wall-hung shelf to hold mail, with a small turquoise leather bench shoved beneath it for sitting on during boot removal.)

The living room had tones of creamy beiges, whites and off-whites, brilliant turquoise, and black. Brasses glittered on the round cocktail table. Re-covered, the couch was almost a piece of artwork: a Persian print combining all the colors of the room.

Three chairs gathered round it—exclamation points of black tufted antique satin on brass wheels. (Antique satin is neither antique nor satin; it is silky, nubby, infinitely easy to upholster with, and seems to wear forever.)

Lew's chair and ottoman angled in front of his redone desk. They were covered in the same bold fabric as the couch, and were lit by the lamp on the desk, which held a new beige leather desk set, paperweights of vari-sized turquoise glass—even the large writing blotter was that same brilliant blue.

Everywhere you looked there was soft light touching a piece of white or turquoise porcelain, or glancing off a bright brass object. Plants seemed to flourish in the room, as well as out of doors. The picture window, framed in the fascinating couch fabric—its ribbon-like blinds closed or not—was a picture win-dow, indeed.

The Stuck-in-the-House Wife

You walked through to the dining room and the turquoise was there, too. On the wallpaper. Now it was joined by gold color on the chair seats, a shining brass chandelier, many plants. A big, framed mirror reflected the whole living room again. The black-and-white vinyl floor gleamed.

The house was open. The den seemed quiet, but if you opened its doors, someone was there. Browns in this room, turquoise again, the small new sofa in lemon yellow.

You walked around the house and found its occupants in every room. Some with doors open, some with doors shut. Each had his own place. But the whole house was free to use.

Thea, luxuriating on her chaise longue, glancing around the uncluttered bedroom that seemed to have sprouted coral-tinted flowers and green leaves, was laughing. She had just hung up the phone.

"That was Lew," she said, still laughing. "He's coming home early, with a group of horse brasses. . . . I misunderstood what he was talking about."

(Wonderful. Her laughter was worthy of a collection.)

Lew, the collector, was proud.

And Thea was no longer envious of other people's houses. We had gone together to see some of them. That's how I discovered that turquoise was her color. She had thought she was coveting ancient Persian porcelains, costly French Sèvres pieces. What really was captivating her was their color.

Envy used correctly becomes admiration. You can emulate whatever you admire.

Exit

Decorating is optical illusion. I realize it more and more. The women I've worked with who have had to make emotional moves—the terrible moves—have proved it to me. And to themselves, as well. When all the traumas had been faced, the decisions made, the furniture placed, we had succeeded, together, to make a new or an old place *seem* completely different. Larger than it was, somehow. Lighter, perhaps, than reality would find it. Optical illusion is a kind of magic. It is the magic of putting six roses in front of a mirror and finding yourself, suddenly, with a dozen roses.

But before any illusion can be achieved, reality has to be faced. Facing reality takes the courage of the classical dreamer, the dreamer who makes things happen even when they seem impossible. All the women you have met in this book had problems and they had dreams. But, armed with facts and the ability to cope, they were able to take their fantasies and turn them into practical reality. Each one came out better than she had been before. Even if she had suffered tangible losses, she gained by making her move well. The "terrible moves"? Well, they actually were not so terrible. After they were done, they turned out to have been wonderful moves.

Exit

Still, there is a very strange period after a big move has been made. It is the time when you look around your new house and become critical. Your refreshed eyes begin to question some of the carefully chosen items. You wonder whether that particular chair should have been done in blue instead of gold; whether that ashtray should have been a larger, brass one, or perhaps a small silver one.

Showing your house for the first time becomes to you as important as the opening of a Broadway show. Well, I'd suggest you feel that way for approximately the length of one act, and then take a very long intermission. This is the time to remember that you can always second-guess your own or someone else's work. If your house were really perfect in every detail, I honestly think it would be a very dull place.

So when it has weathered its first criticism and you're relaxed enough, settle back in your seat and realize you've produced a hit. And how do you know? Because you're in it, and you feel a new sensation in it. It's called pleasure. The pleasure that comes from remembering that you made the move or the changes because something had been very wrong. And now, somehow, it isn't. If there are flaws remaining, they can be compared to laugh lines. They come to us all from smiling.

Those big decisions about throwing things away, all those recently lost objects—they will become vague memories. If you choose to look back, you will see that all you have really lost is anguish, because you will have lost the pattern that caused it. The woman who finds herself living in a new house—created because it *had* to be—will find that she is a new woman. She has acquired more patience, she is more experimental; she's able to rearrange, to redo, and to make do. She has grown a little older and she has acquired more wisdom. The wisdom has made her face her big change, has made her able to accept the fact that she can't and probably shouldn't change everything. So this

223

new woman in her new house finds it easier to make adjustments.

Every decision she made was not only based on necessity, but was also backed by the desire to please herself and the people around her. And there will be people around her. I've seen it happen so many times. A house is as full and lively as the lady who lives in it. It will reflect her. But, unlike those six roses that suddenly become twelve, the change in her is no illusion.

And when you've changed your house *and* yourself, what *do* you do with the bed? You stop crying in it. A bed is for rest, for pleasure, for greeting the morning happily. That's the whole idea. Heaven comes later.